ST. LEO'S CHURCH

Leo High School

Every Heart and Hand

A Leo High School Story

By

Pat Hickey

authorHOUSE™

1663 LIBERTY DRIVE, SUITE 200
BLOOMINGTON, INDIANA 47403
(800) 839-8640
WWW.AUTHORHOUSE.COM

First published by AuthorHouse 10/03/05

ISBN: 1-4208-5651-0 (sc)

Printed in the United States of America
Bloomington, Indiana

This book is printed on acid-free paper.

Foreward

It truly is, as one Leo teacher called it a few years ago, "The jewel of 79th Street." Step inside the hulking wrought iron gates and the bleak realities of urban life - the guns and the drugs and the creed that you shouldn't want things any better than they already are - gives way to the durability of the American dream.

Leo High is, above and beyond anything else, a place of remarkable achievement. Single mothers scratch together tuition money and string together time to allow their sons to walk the polished corridors festooned with banners that constantly tell them that success is within their reach.

The faculty bats away the notion that such kids of the city are unreachable, and instead carefully guides them toward remarkable scholastic and athletic feats. The successful alumni trample across racial, ethnic, and economic boundaries to help kids who look nothing like them, yet harbor the same quiet ambitions that never change with time.

It is a place unlike any other, a place that not only withstands adversity, but prospers in the face of it. It is a place that believes not only in God, but in itself and every single person fortunate enough to be a part of that great enterprise. Long live Leo High.

By Brian McGrory,

Boston Globe Columnist

Introduction:

'For with every heart and hand, We will fight as one strong band, For the honor of the Orange and Black.'

Oh, when Those Leo Men fall into line,

And Their Colors Black and Orange are Unfurled,

You see those brawny stalwarts wait the sign,

And their might against the foe is hurled.

For then the foe shall feel the lions might,

And the Spirit of our Team's attack,

For with every Heart and Hand,

We will fight as one strong band,

For the honor of the Orange and Black!   Rah! Rah! (Repeat)

(To the melody of the Washington & Lee Fight song)

The Leo School song concludes with a covenant fulfilled for generations. Seventy-six years at this writing and going. It's just after seven AM, and I have completed an Alumni update of lost addresses sent in by Jim Coogan '44. Jim is a retired plumber, but a full-stride Leo man.

I get about six updates a month from Jim by mail or passed on at a Leo home game.

My name is Pat Hickey and I help raise money for Leo High School. I was raised in this neighborhood, but did not attend Leo. I went to Little Flower High School one mile to the west on 79th Street. Little Flower High School was a parish school. It and the parish itself are now closed. It has been my privilege to work here for the last ten years. Previously I was a teacher and Director of Development at Catholic schools in Indiana and at Bishop McNamara High School in Kankakee, Illinois. It was there that a beautiful skinny red-headed Art teacher, Mary Cleary, married me and we partnered at Bishop Mac and went halves on three wonderful children. My wife, Mary, died of a brain tumor during my second year at Leo. I moved my three children back to Chicago. They are now south siders. Now, back to the Leo High School story.

Outside of my cubicle on the first floor, President Bob Foster is talking to Mrs. Verna Lynch about errors in a phone billing and Ms Natasha Adams, the President's secretary types letters to Mr. Tom Zbierski concerning the recipients of Cardinal Bernardin Scholarship of The Big Shoulders Fund and the two receptions that they are to attend. Upstairs, Illinois State Champion Track Coaches Ed Adams and Brother John "Steve" O'Keefe CFC are putting together the day's attendance lists which will be returned to the first floor where Bonita Simmons, Leo technology coordinator, will do the updates, while Stacey Redmond, Leo's registrar doubles on the phones and Chiquita Body takes care of student tuition payment. Bonita pulls a transcript for Jason McDonald '03 who is taking the apprenticeship exam for Pipe –Fitters Local 597. Jason hopes to follow Lonnie Newman '01 in the trades. Lonnie turned down six scholarships to join the pipe-fitters. Lonnie is their top apprentice. LaToya Wade keeps the coffee going and sorts a mailing. Head Custodian Ronnell Reynolds appears and vanishes all over the school and keeps in contact with the Main Office and President Foster by cell phone and walkie-talkie. The Office normally welcomes about four or five parents through the morning, dropping off tuition or checking up on a student's progress with Principal Bob Kman or schedule changes with Vice Principal Larry Kennelly. Student Office workers dart up and down the stairs with messages to and from Dean Dan O'Keefe who handles tardiness, dress code, attitude, and locker issues, while monitoring the security cameras on the Halls.

The cameras can be sure to pick –up Mike Joyce'86 dropping off boxing equipment from Martin and Ollie Mc Garry to Leo's 2nd Floor Boxing facility on his way to the County Building. Mike helped revive Leo Boxing that flourished in the 1970's and 80's under Bob Galloway CPD. Mike is an attorney and works with Cook County States Attorney Dick Devine's STAY Program that encourages high school kids to avoid gangs and drugs. Along with Bob Foster, Mike Joyce is one of the smartest people I have ever met – and that includes the late genius, Steve Allen, who originated the Tonight Show, wrote over 5,000 songs, recorded jazz albums, and some of the greatest jokes in American humor. I got to know Steve Allen over three days when he agreed to do a fund raiser for no fee, when I worked at Bishop Noll Institute in Hammond, Indiana. Steve Allen, by the way, was kicked out of Mount Carmel in his freshman year and ended up at Hyde Park High School. Mike Joyce lives simply and works to help hundreds of people. I am no longer stunned by the number, quality, diversity, and integrity of people on Mike's speed dial. One minute he's talking to Fight Trainer Kevin Rooney, Then a call to Heavyweight Boxer and Leo Grad Tommy Hayes, the next Steve Neal of the Sun Times, the next, a call from NBC Sportscaster Peggy Kusinzki, the next John Kerry's

Campaign, the next Plumber Terry Cox, finally Mrs. Virginia McCaskey (The Real Mamma Bear) and then without a breath he picks up in the middle of our talk about Bishop Sheil.

Dr. Jack O'Keefe '59 of Daley College and Leo Alumnus Denny Conway '62 are on the fourth floor to conduct SAT/ACT Prep Classes. Catholic school veteran teachers like Bob Shablaske can be seen shooing guys to class before the bell and three hundred Leo students settle into classes on the top three floors of Leo. African American Leo graduates comprise one third of Leo's teaching staff; giving back to the school that gave to them: Otto Horton '93, Barry Israel '94, Jerry Newell '72 Noah Cannon '95. Jackie Gilmer, Earl Harris, and James Crawford who maintain Leo's physical plant can be seen on every floor through the day. George Newell '83 is Leo's beat cop from the Sixth District. Alumni Association President Jack Howard '61 has driven into the parking lot to deliver Alumni license plate covers designed by Bob Sigel '54. These will be given to Alumni visitors. Earl goes out the old chapel door and helps Jack with the boxes.

Through all of this activity, Bob Foster has gotten a call from Frank Considine '39 and heads to his office doling out compliments to Mrs. Barbara Simmons who drives the bus to the southwest suburbs and Coaches Leo's Bowling Team. Al Townsend, whose sons attended Leo and now maintains Leo's motor pool, delays Foster's access to the phone with a request for bus parts. Foster takes Considine's call and learns that Leo's Director of Development's Fax with the current addresses of the Considine Scholars has not gone through and this narrative is halted. . . .

The story of Leo High School is the story of courageous, committed people: 'every Heart and Hand.' They are people with the courage to give back to a school that helped to develop their character as Christian citizens and with the commitment to overlook race and religion as factors in making that financial and moral support. This is more of a thank you letter than it is a history. It is also a wake up call to the African American community. Leo High School needs the support of all people who value education and the future success of young men in Chicago. Over the last twelve years, hundreds of African American young men received a college preparatory education because of the joint efforts of their families and white Catholic Alumni. Leo High School at the turn of this century serves 300 African American young men on the south side of Chicago. Today only one of ten Leo students claims to be Catholic. At its openning in 1926, all students were Catholic and all were white. There is a powerful spirit uniting the generations and that is the Spirit of the Lion.

Leo High School is the home to many men, powerful and prominent in Chicago, in Illinois and the Nation –Bishop John R. Gorman, Andy McKenna, Illinois Justice Thomas Fitzgerald, Don Flynn, Frank Considine & etc. Here's but a few:

Edward Joyce '70 – President Chicago Board of Options Exchange
Terrence Duffy '72 – CEO Chicago Mercantile Exchange
Michael McErlean '74- President Eurex American Division
James T. Joyce '60- Commissioner Chicago Fire Department
James J. Molloy '69 – Chief of Detectives Chicago Police Department
Thomas D. Stokes '54 – CEO Interstate Electronics Company
William J. Koloseike '45 – CEO Bill Kay Chrysler & Dodge
Gerard J. Haggerty '56 – CEO Haggerty Chevrolet
Kenny Philpot '97 – Detroit Lions
Chris Watson '95 – Buffalo Bills
Harold Blackmon '95 – Seattle Seahawks

John Linehan '73 – VP for Investments Prudential Investments, Inc.
Bill Holland '72 – VP Gallagher Midwest
Jason Jefferson '00 - New Orleans Saints
Jack Hallberg '59 – CEO J. Hallberg Agency
James Hallberg '69 – CEO Insure One, Inc.
Fr. William Joseph McFarlane '83 – Archdiocese of Chicago
Joseph Mulhern '38 – Chicago Law Legend
John Hector '72 – Editor Daily Southtown
Joseph A. Power '70 – Partner Power, Rogers, & Smith
E. Michael Kelly '65 – Partner Hinshaw & Culbertson
Patrick F. Daly '67 – CEO Daly Group Architects
Daniel McGrath '68 – Sports Editor Chicago Tribune
Steve Lattimore '81 – Correspondent CBS News
Rev. John Sullivan '68 – Chaplain Illinois State Police
Lt. Gen. George Muellner USAF (ret)'61 –President Boeing Corp.'s Strategic Defense Systems Division & Phantom Works.
H. Richard Landis '47-CEO Landis Plastics Inc.
Dr. Stafford Hood '70 – Dean of Educational Psychology Arizona State University
Richard Finn'71- Director Boeing Corp. Midwest Capital Corporation
John Q. O'Donnell '68, Principal, Partner &Chief Financial Officer, The John Buck Company

These men came from families of modest means. Most were the sons of firemen, policemen, streetcar and bus drivers, tradesmen, and semi-skilled laborers. While Auburn Gresham was a comfortable community it certainly was not a Winnetka or Kenilworth. It was a home for families on the way up in American life. One generation removed from the slums and rising. The neighborhood produced fighters who take it.

Andy McKenna
- 1947

One of Chicago's top lawyers, Mike Kelly '65, passed to Heaven in August of 2004. The week before he died Chicago Magazine ran an article that featured an attorney at the pinnacle of his trade – attorney for Sheriff Michael Sheahan, Father Michael Pfleger, Sox & Bulls owner Jerry Reinsdorf, co- founder of the Nellie Fox Society and partner in Hinshaw and Culbertson LLP. Mike was a pit bull with a sense of humor. He bit onto challenges. As a football

Justice Thomas Fitzgerald '59

player at Leo, Mike mirrored the Chicago Catholic League itself – undersized and overachieving. At 5'9" Mike Kelly hardly seemed a block of granite destined for NCAA football, as a lineman. He was recruited by Alabama's Bear Bryant but deferred when Bryant's freshman football academic program would not allow him to study pre-law. Mike went on to play at Michigan State, graduated and chomped his way through Northwestern Law. When my wife was suffering in her last days, Mike called me nearly every day to see how I was holding up. Here was a partner for a blue-stocking Chicago Law Firm cutting into his day to see if someone else needed help. Mike supported several students at Leo with financial aid. Mike always referred to himself as' a poor kid from St. Brendan's who had a lot of help. E. Michael Kelly is your average Leo Man from the neighborhood.

Today Auburn Gresham struggles against urban decay and community anchors like Leo High School helped to gain an upper-hand in the struggle. Students of Leo High School come from the same two-

Frank Considine & Cardinal George

flats and bungalows as their spiritual forefathers, but the realities facing them go beyond poverty itself. A sub-culture that disdains academic success is more than simply hostile to them. Getting to and from school is a life and death matter. These kids have to fight their way through the gang-bangers, literally and figuratively. They need people who are committed to making a better world and those people can be found in the Leo Alumni Directory.

Jack Fitzgerald
'69 Coach &
Teacher

These young Lions continue to astonish Chicago. Since 1991, 93% of Leo High school graduates have been accepted in colleges and universities. The 2003 Salutatorian won an appointment to West Point. The President of Quincy University's Student Body for 2004, Jamal Thompson, is a Leo Man. Chicago Police Tactical Officer Eric Lee ('81) was killed in the line of duty in 2001. Five of his teammates from the 1981 Track team are also Chicago Police Officers. These young men are part of a great tradition of courage and commitment.

Since 1981, Leo High School has won Five IHSA State Track Championships in both Class A and Class AA. Leo High School is the only Catholic high school to win the State of Illinois Track Title in its 110 year history. Leo graduates play in the NFL and are highly visible in NCAA sports. Leo has a tradition of great competitive spirit. More importantly there is a spirit of giving back that must be understood and re-ignited. Though African American's have graduated from Leo for nearly forty years, Black

'60 James Joyce

1952, Jim
Corbett

Alumni support accounts for less than one percent of annual contributions. This is a problem that Black Alumni leaders like Ben DeBerry ('65), Stafford Hood ('70), William Payne ('75) and several others have tried to reverse. *Chicago Sun Times* columnist Mary Mitchell broached this subject in a 1996 column. Some reasons for the failure of Black Alumni to respond to Leo High School's needs have been attributed to the racism they experienced while students here in '60s, '70s, and '80s. However, there are no white students at Leo, nor have there been any since 1991. That racial canard is unfair to the Black students at Leo – they need Leo Alumni support – its time for all Leo men to lend heart and hand.

Since 1991, Leo High School has been one hundred percent African American. The neighborhood had become characterized by gang violence, prostitution, and drug traffic. Leo High School continued to anchor the community and offer a beacon of hope. The school serves as a safe haven for its students and an emblem respected by the entire community. Something of value – something positive - continued at 7901 Sangamon.

There is still plenty going on at Leo High School. If it were not for Leo's Alumni hundreds of African American kids would have missed the chance to go on to University of Chicago, Notre Dame, DePaul, Purdue, Wisconsin, Iowa, or Boston College. The reason for this connection can be found in the values of the Catholic parish. Leo men have won appointments to United States Military Academies.

1950 Edward Grant

1947 Dick
Landis

Leo High School continues its mission because of Alumni support. Why do Leo Alumni support an all Black school? What do they gain? What do they get out of it? What's their angle? Who are these people?

There was a place, which had been sold by the Archdiocese of Chicago to the Chicago Board of Education that seems a metaphor of the Leo Spirit. It is now the athletic field of Amos Alonzo Stagg Grammar School. In 1927 it was owned by St. Leo the Great Parish. This might be a good place to begin to understand the nature of the people who have kept this inner city school alive and fixed to its mission. Let's begin in the fall of 1962.

Shewbridge Field was named for Monsignor Peter F. Shewbridge, the Pastor of St. Leo's Parish and the founder of Leo High School. At one time this remarkable stadium at 74th & Aberdeen Streets in Chicago was called Molloy Field and owned by the same family. Pastor Shewbridge bought the property for the use and benefit of Leo High School. The stadium would be used by the Gaelic Athletic Association (GAA) in the late 1950's & '60's and in 1948 would be the home of the All-American Girls Professional Baseball League's Chicago Colleens. The Marquette Bloomer Girls 16" Softball Team used Shewbridge in the 1950's. Lastly, Shewbridge is memorable as the Chicago stop for Donkey Baseball in the 1940's & 50's. The revenue generated by use of

1944-1947 Oriole Rev Mons. Shewbridge

JUBILARIAN

1944-1947 Oriole Rev
Brother Daly 1945

the stadium went to the benefit of St. Leo Parish and Leo High School. Shewbridge Field was a neighborhood community landmark –today we would call it a cultural icon. On its turf some of the most vicious and inspiring football games were –not played – slugged out.

For Chicago, in the fall of 1962, the single most influential community institutions were the Roman Catholic parishes. The spires of the Catholic Churches were the identity of the many neighborhoods. Anyone who has traveled the Dan Ryan Expressway notes the old St. Martin's gothic dominance of the west lane landscape. Looking in any direction from the passage ramps at the, God forgive me, U.S. Cellular Field (Comiskey Park) one recognizes the dominance of the churches. They were *National* (German, Polish, Czech, Italian, French, or Lithuanian language and membership) Parishes or *Territorial* (English language) parishes. However, until the mid-1960's the language of the liturgy was that of the universal Catholic Church – Latin. The American Catholic Church evolved as a schizophrenic entity social & economic liberalism joined at the hip by ecclesiastical conservatism: a priest might get his head split on a picket line but would autocratically enforce a strict moral and theological control over his flock. The Organization of Southwest Communities, Catholic Youth Organization, and the Legion

1944 Tom Driscoll

1938 J. B.
Hartney

of Decency all enjoyed the imprimatur of the same Archbishop.

A Roman Catholic was in the White House and the Leo football line-up consisted of names that our Dads and our uncles bragged about at Lou's on Ashland or the Wooden House on 79th Street. Leo had won nine Catholic League Championships and three City Titles in football. The name of Shewbridge Field might spark an image of the Lion in the minds of hundreds of Leo men and those who faced them. This spirit of the Lion – dignified, courageous, and indomitable – is arguably evident in defeat as well as triumph.

Leo Coach Bob Hanlon had just taken over from the legendary Jimmy Arneberg, who had won Leo's 1956 City Championship. Hanlon's Lions had blanked '61/'62 City Champ Mount Carmel 26-0 and beaten Mendel, Loyola, and Brother Rice. The looming battle with St. Rita High School under Coach Buckley was a very big deal! Shewbridge was packed and everyone was charged up for the brawl to come.

It was Leo's Tom Donnellan who scored first and Mike Johnson's extra point made it 7-0. But St. Rita came back with a great 67 yard run followed by a two point conversion. After that it was pure Chicago Catholic League mud and blood. These guys really pounded on each other until the fourth quarter when St. Rita broke Leo's defensive wall adding 8 more points to the total. Leo intercepted late in the game but time ran out. St. Rita 16; Leo 7.

Frank
Considine '39

1935
Shewbridge
Msgr

The 1962/63 Leo Team went on to win the next three games before losing to a powerful Fenwick squad in the Catholic League Championship at Soldier Field. Shewbridge Field and Leo High School represented the people who built them. They were institutional crucibles for the raw products of success – Courage and Commitment.

The people who built Leo High School are the people who continue to support Leo. They are the bloodied and bruised guys who had to face Coaches Bob Hanlon, Tony Kelly, and Bob Swazt after losing to St. Rita. There are thousands of them. They moved out of the neighborhoods around Leo. They continue to be scorned as intolerant and clannish, but they send hundreds of thousands of dollars back to a school in the old neighborhood serving young men of a different race and religion. Why is that?

Leo High School's reputation, enrollment and financial health had weakened the Lion's roar by 1990. Then, in what seemed to be the death blow to the school, in 1991 The Congregation of Christian Brothers (Christian Brothers of Ireland) ended their commitment to Leo High School.

Fortunately, one Leo man who was present at that game in 1962 became the first lay leader of this great school in 1991 and the Alumni stepped up to breathe new spirit into the old Lion. Robert W. Foster, a 1958 Leo man, member of the 1956 City Championship Team, Purdue University football star and graduate, was freshman football coach at Leo during the 1962/63

1931 Red
Gleason

season and a well respected social studies teacher at Leo High School. He is the corporeal link to Leo High School's Catholic culture and the success of today's Leo man. Bob Foster is the bridge to this school's identity and the channel of financial support from the white Alumni.

While the varsity suffered defeat that day, the 1962 Leo Freshman Football team that included the great Coe Francis, Jerry Prosser, Wally Scahill, and Jay Standring would enjoy an undefeated season. This team would go on to play Loyola in the 1965 Prep Bowl. But Foster would be coaching at Little Flower High School one mile west of Leo. Foster gave Little Flower its first winning season and recruited such stand-out athletes as Jim McMahon, Gene Monahan, Mike Thomas, Mark Williams, John Rank, and Bill Richardson. Twenty-nine years later, in 1991, Foster would step in to lead Leo High School. Foster toughened his values of courage and commitment at Shewbridge Field and in the classrooms of Leo High School. Like the thousands of Leo men before him, those values were seeded in the home, nurtured in Catholic schools, and shared with others. Foster is a product of those who have gone before him.

They are the same people who built St. Leo, Sacred Heart, St. Brendan's, St. Columbanus, Our Lady of Mount Carmel, St. Sabina's, St. Felicitas, and Little Flower parishes. They built the many great Catholic high schools that once crammed the urban landscape. The racial balance in Chicago, especially on the south side, shifted from the 1960's on. The quest for

fair housing by African American families became a cynical windfall for unprincipled real estate sharks – blacks and whites were fleeced and further polarized. Academics and the media spat out 'white flight' as code for ethnic Catholic bigotry. The racial card became a trump that would continue

1931 Ike Mahoney

to favor the charlatan. Racism is a cancer but too many quacks have been allowed to probe its roots. The race baiters and the bigots keep the body politic infected with rhetoric: the words that smear, hurt and divide.

Nevertheless, a common thread binds the history of Leo and is found in its motto FACTA NON VERBA – Deeds Not Words. The evidence ironically enough is found in the written words and sentiments of Leo students. The values intended to take root in the students flower out from the yellowed and dusty pages of *The Oriole*, Leo High School's student newspaper. *The Oriole's* regular features included news (world, local, school, and interscholastic), sports, essays, book reviews, and a full page dedicated to Catholic activities and interests. Mr. Paul Somers '46 author of *The Lake Michigan Aircraft Carriers* earned a great reputation as editor of the Leo newspaper, while working for Enrico Fermi's team at the University of Chicago – Paul was a clerk for the Physics Library. The Faith of Leo students was always in the forefront.

As one primary source for our consideration, this student run paper is a trove for insight to the nature of the Leo spirit. This spirit is best made manifest in the powerful financial support of Alumni and the continued achievement of Leo students in the new millennium. The spirit of the lion is reflected in the editorial of November 8th, 1938 Edition of *The Oriole*, by J. B. Hartney '39:

> Does a ghost haunt the corridors of Leo? Is our once majestic school spirit now nothing but a fitful flitting phosphorescent figure? We don't think so! The Leo Lion's tail is still unknotted. Bloodied but unbowed he roars defiance to those who would subdue him. Halted? Yes! Conquered? No! His head is up, his fangs are bared. Temporarily subdued, yet he remains a danger to those who would destroy him. They know his strength, and face him not too boldly. But he is hurt,

and yet may fall before their rush, unless they give him aid. It is to us that he must look for help. Our cheers will give him courage. *Our support will give him strength.*

It is not alone on the gridiron that the Lion needs aid. *We must encourage and support him in all school activities as have our predecessors. We are indebted to him. We owe him our support.* For years he has kept the name of Leo ahead, and now he grows weary. , shall we desert him to his fate? *Let us rally behind him and show him we still believe in his ability to keep Leo out front.* (Emphasis my own)

J.B. Hartney graduated from Loyola Medical School in 1945. In 1958, Dr. James Hartney conducted the blood analyses for the victims of the Holy Angels fire as chief pathologist for St. Anne Hospital. St. Anne's blood lab normally conducted no more than 100 such tests per month. In three days Dr. Hartney conducted 300 tests. Of the 80 horribly burned children admitted to St. Anne, only three perished. Some years later, Dr. Hartney suffered a scalpel cut during a procedure – he was infected with hepatitis. There was no known treatment at the time, but Dr. Hartney kept a journal of his experimental therapies until his death. His records were published in *The American Journal of Medicine*- hepatitis can now be treated. He lived the Spirit of the Lion.

Leo High School flourishes – without subsidies from the Archdiocese of Chicago, nor the support of African American businesses and private foundations, without the sponsorship of the Christian Brothers , – because guys - who grew up amid the brick yards, lumber yards, tile yards, coal yards, and steel fabricators, established lives formed by values that honor courage and commitment - give back. They give out of love for their fellow man. These tough taciturn men love young black kids who face a much tougher world than they suppose they did. These guys would never articulate such a sentiment – ever – and so it falls to this outsider to give their hearts some voice.

In the act of giving back, people build the future. Joseph Mulhern '38 declined induction to Leo's Hall of Fame in 2004 because the tens of thousands of dollars he contributes to help poor kids get an education is 'not such a big deal.' The magnificent churches and schools of Catholic Chicago did not come about by osmosis. They were built by immigrants and the children of immigrants - people of intense faith but modest means. They gave pennies and nickels to build the first wooden frame St. Leo Church in 1885 at a cost of $ 50,000 and in 1901 spent much more to replace it with a beautiful Romanesque Church.

Catholics built schools close to their Churches to further the Faith of their children and their children's children. They built hospitals, schools, and social services. They bought land for future development. The most successful parishioners reached back to the parishes from their financial comforts in order to help the neediest. Courage and Commitment was the core curriculum in Catholic homes and the schools. Faith without Action was not a Catholic tenet. In "What Parish Are You From, ?" Professor Eileen McMahon states that the" Devotional life permeated Catholic life." Catholics participate in Novenas of Our Lady of Sorrows, Sacred Heart, St. Jude, the Rosary (150 Hail Marys, 15 Our Fathers, 15 meditations of the life and passion of Jesus) and Devotions of the Liturgical year are reflected throughout the pages of The Oriole in testimony to the powerful impact on the spiritual growth of Leo men. This devotion is reflected in no small way to the active support for the school. Leo High School reflected the values that built the Archdiocese of Chicago.

In *The 1936 Lion*, published ten years after the dedication of Leo High School by Cardinal Mundelein, Leo's student editor, Walter Kahl, wrote

> We, the senior class, dedicate this sixth edition of the Lion to the founders of Leo High School. . . . Ten short years ago, Brothers Doorley, Grangel, O'Donnell and Filehne came to Chicago and set to work to establish an Irish Christian Brothers' school in the Midwest. Uppermost in their minds was the desire to bring to Catholic youth the principles that the Irish Christian Brothers stand for – training in Religion and Morals. Under their guidance Leo quickly gained the name and prestige it now maintains.

> Therefore, let us, the class of 1936, and all our successors do our utmost to preserve and increase the glory of Leo which was sown by these beloved servants of God.

The 1936 Lion also noted the establishment of The Leo Alumni Association which continues its support of Leo High School. Leo Baseball Great, Al Mahieu '35 served the Association for Seven Decades. Six years after the first class graduated from Leo, Alumni organized a dance at the Medina Athletic Club for benefit of Leo High School. Immediately Leo men acted to give back to the school. Courage and Commitment had become manifest in the two hundred graduates of Leo's first five years.

In 2003, Leo's Alumni and the Alumni Association gave back more than $ 300,000 to the school's operations. In 2003 Leo High School has no debt, operates on a zero-deficit, balanced budget and enjoys the support of its Alumni. This is a story that needs telling and I pray for the grace to do justice to Leo High School's story.

In a few chapters, I'd like to try and solder the connections between Leo High School's current status as a great Catholic high school serving African American young men, most of whom are non-Catholic, and the foundation of the school as an opportunity for young men to succeed as Catholic Americans. My narrative will jump around chronologically in support of the theme of this story: courage and commitment. One thing that I will do is miss to mention some great Leo Man and for that I apologize – my Dad always said I couldn't find my butt with both hands. You, the un-named, are a big part of this story. It is the combination of courage and commitment so strongly enforced in the Leo education that continues to this day. Leo High School has been down but never out. It has undergone dramatic changes all in the spirit of The Lion.

79th & Halsted North View

MAN OF THE MONTH

DEANE WAS ELECTED PRESIDENT OF 4C BY HIS CLASSMATES

Deane Thomas

AS CAPTAIN DEANE REPRESENTS THE TEAM IN DEALINGS WITH THE REF.

Oriole Man of the Month 1945

Man of the Year Dick Prendergast Class of 43 and
Jack Howard presenting the award

Table of Contents

THE ORIOLE STAFF

SITTING: WILLIAM SHEFCIK, WILLIAM VONDER HEIDE, ANDREW PLACCO, EDITOR 1945, ROBERT DEVANE, EDITOR 1944, ROBERT HYLARD, REV. BROTHER P. B. CROKE, MODERATOR JOHN SHEFCIK. STANDING: ANDREW MC KENNA, CHARLES REILLY, JOSEPH LINEHAN WILLIAM KURTZ, PATRICK MOORE, JAMES SHANNON, PAUL SOMERS, JAMES WHITE, DON-ALD LAW, DAVID MCNAMARA.

I. Catholic Chicago – A Snapshot of Leo High School's Origins

Here in Chicago, the visible Church staggers the imagination. In Bridgeport alone, a neighborhood of one and one & ½ miles square, there were ten Catholic Churches serving five different ethnic groups (Spinney p. 143). Catholics were not alone in this phenomenon as there were Baptist Churches conducted in thirteen different languages. However, Catholics were stamped with the stigmata of "the unassimilated and foreign." The 1868 rant in the *Chicago Evening Post that*

> The Country has survived the Irish emigration – the worst with which any other country was afflicted. The Irish fill our prisons, our reform schools, our hospitals. . . . Scratch a convict or a pauper and the chances are that you tickle the skin of an Irish Catholic . . . made a criminal or a pauper by the priest and politician who have deceived him and kept him in ignorance, in a word, a savage, as he was born (76)

ignores the fact that one third of Chicago's Union Army composition was Irish Catholic. The Irish and the Germans, many whom were also Roman Catholic, volunteered. Though these Union Army soldiers were mostly Copperheads –Democrats and opposed to the Civil War largely because immigrants were doing the most of the dying –they were loyal to their adopted country. In *Bygone Days* it is noted that whenever there was Union victory, celebrations broke out on the North side, but Bridgeport seemed to celebrate only Rebel victories. Unwilling to be maintained in the public imagination as outsiders, Catholics in Chicago courageously committed to making their mark in the commercial and cultural life of their city.

Among them, a forgotten Catholic American, Sen. James Shields (1806-1879) came to America from Ireland and settled in Illinois. His life-long public service beginning as Illinois Auditor General often found him at opposites with Abraham Lincoln, as political rivals. Honest Abe, lampooned the young Shields in the Whig Sangamon Journal in 1842. Shields had fought in the Florida Wars upon coming to America in 1823 and called Lincoln out for a duel. At the last minute, Lincoln apologized publicly and the matter remained a life-long source of embarrassment for the Great Emancipator. This Democrat, Shields organized the Illinois Volunteer Regiment for the Mexican War, was wounded twice at Cerro Gordo, Chapultepec and personally raised the American flag at the siege of Mexico City, while Lincoln the Whig opposed the war in Congress. The Illinois Catholic returned to the Senate and was defeated in 1855 after the Kansas- Nebraska Act was signed into law, when Lincoln urged his supporters to back Lyman Trumbull, who jumped back and forth between parties. That tactic cleared the path to the White House for our 16th President. Ironically, much of what Lincoln argued in his Great Debate with Douglas can be found in Shields' 1850 address to Congress on admission of California as a free state.

Shields moved to Minnesota and helped bring that territory into the Union and when the Civil War began was appointed Brigadier General by his old Illinois nemesis. It is interesting that the "rail-splitter" appointed Democrats to military posts – talk about clever censorship. Gen. Shields was the only Federal officer during the war to defeat Thomas "Stonewall" Jackson, which Shields accomplished at the battle of Kernstown in the Shenandoah Valley campaign. Again wounded in the service of his country, Shields resigned from the Army of the Potomac after Lincoln tried to promote him to major general. The arch-Republican Sec. of War Stanton objected to too many victorious Catholic Democratic Union Generals (notably Phil Sheridan & William Rosecrans). Shields went on to serve in the Senate for Missouri and helped attract Catholic emigrants to Iowa. Sen. James Shields died in Ottumwa, IA on Jan. 1st, 1879. The two men who represent Illinois in the Congressional Statuary Hall are Lincoln & Shields. Most of us south siders only recognized Shields as the street home to the Chicago White Sox.

James Shields told America's leading Churchman in the 1860's, Archbishop John Hughes of New York, something that Catholic churchmen too often forget, "The trouble is that YOU think you build churches, but you do not . . . The people, the   parishioners, the businessmen, the mechanics, the laborers and hired girls, with their savings, build them, and no others." (146-155 Schauniger) Would that our clergy could remember that.

Senator James Shields, veteran of the Florida Wars, French speaking Illinois auditor General who kept Illinois solvent during the 1837 Panic, nearly fought a duel with Abraham Lincoln, who backed down, key proponent of the Illinois Central Railroad, hero of Cerro Gordo, Chapultepec, Mexico City, Kernstown; Senator of Illinois

3

and 1st Senator of Minnesota, and Senator for Missouri, key member of the group that brought California into the Union as a Free State might deserve some up to date recognition.

A sad truth, try to find anything about this great Catholic American in a US History text or in Bill Gates' Microsoft Encyclopedia. James Shields, like the people who built Catholic Chicago is ignored or edited out. Like the Leo Man who goes unprinted in my pages here, Shields deeds were more important than what was said about him. He has a part in Leo's History. His courage and commitment are testimony to the vitality of Catholic values.

It must be noted here that Catholic Chicagoans were few in 1833 when the first Catholic priest to establish a church in this area, Father St. Cyr arrived from St. Louis. One hundred and twenty-eight Chicago Catholics petitioned Bishop Rosati for a permanent parish. Most were French and the document sent to the Ordinary of St. Louis was written in French. The first Catholic Church in Chicago was built on the south west corner of State & Lake – St. Mary's. The Church was later moved to a site on Madison Ave. between Wabash & State, where it would remain until swept up in the Great Chicago Fire of 1871. By 1837, the Catholic population swelled to 3,000 with the arrival of Irish canal diggers. Then in 1843 The Fifth Provincial Council of Baltimore erected the establishment of the diocese of Chicago and its first bishop Rt. Rev. William Quarter.

Bishop Quarter directed his See from a frontier village parish into a diocese with a Cathedral, a seminary, a university, and a literary society to augment the growing number of German, Irish, and French parishes. Quarter secured from the Illinois Legislature an act dated December 9, 1844 incorporating The University of St. Mary of the Lake, a mere six months after his arrival. In February 1845, this far-sighted bishop secured from the

Illinois Legislature, The Catholic Bishop of Chicago and his successors a "corporation sole" to hold property in trust for religious purposes. There would be no trustee in this diocese. Bishop Quarter conducted fund-raising missions in the east and in Europe for the propagation of the Chicago diocese.

Having secured an educational institution for males, Bishop Quarter asked the Sisters of Mercy to establish a college for women. Bishop Quarter and his successors (Bishops Van De Velde, O'Regan, Duggan, Foley, Feehan and Quigley) built-up the Chicago Diocese to meet the growing needs of the faithful.

Bishop James Duggan (1858-68) baptized Ex-Governor Bissell and Lincoln's Democratic opponent Stephan A. Douglas into the Catholic faith, as well as directed the Church through the horrors of the Civil War. Bishop Duggan was most responsible for attracting religious Orders of men and women to Chicago to augment the ministry to the ever growing ethnic groups and to provide educational opportunities beyond grammar school (DeLaSalle Institute in 1861 and St. Ignatius in 1870).

Bishop Duggan's successor Bishop Thomas Foley (1870-79) assumed the title of Coadjutor Bishop when Bishop Duggan succumbed to mental illness attributed to the strain of his ministry and the pernicious schism of Pastor Chiniquy in Kankakee County (Chiniquy is the only case in American history of outright apostasy – Chiniquy led hundreds of French parishioners in Kankakee out of the Roman Catholic Church; He became an Anti-Catholic lecturer and author much loved by the anti-immigrant Press). Bishop Foley had barely assumed the role of Catholic Ordinary when on October 9th 1871, from 10 o'clock on Sunday evening to 6'clock on the evening of the following day, . . . afire of quite uncontrollable character spread over Chicago, sweeping the entire

5

business district of the city and thousands of residences and leaving in its wake of destruction a loss in buildings, merchandise and household effects estimated at $ 200,000,000. A great part of the material equipment of the Catholic Church in Chicago in churches, schools, and institutions, representing years of self-sacrificing toil and generosity on the part of clergy and laity, was involved in the common disaster (Garraghan 221).

Bishop Foley is credited with initiating the rebirth of the Diocese from the ashes of disaster:

> Catholic response to the call for help was prompt and generous and in no long time the Catholics of Chicago, under the leadership of the indomitable Bishop Foley, the man of the hour, were heartened to look around them and plan for the restoration of the Church to something of its pristine splendor. (Garraghan 223)

It is interesting to note that the native Anglo-American response to aid for the victims of the Great Fire came in the form of The Relief and Aid Society. This entity was founded on the philosophy of "scientific charity." Applicants for aid were assessed on their 'worthiness.' "Chicagoans who had demonstrated past entrepreneurial zeal and had owned property were most likely to receive aid; chronically poor Chicagoans who could offer no track record of thrift, investment, steady employment, and financial success often got none." (Spinney 105). Most of Bishop Foley's flock fell into that last category. However, Foley sparked a responsive fire that burned into the coming century – a building program that paralleled Chicago's rebirth.

The next fifty years, prelates Feehan and Quigley continued the powerful restoration of Catholic Chicago. Bishop Quigley in particular promoted the educational concerns of the diocese. At the turn of the century, 41% of Chicago's population was foreign born. Between 1880

1920 'about 2.5 million immigrants came to Chicago' (Spivey 123).

Chicago had grown because of foreign immigration and Roman Catholics numbered 262,000 by 1890. The massive immigrations to America in the 19th Century boosted the population of Chicago with German and Irish Catholics. Late in the century Bohemian Czechs, Italians, Lithuanians, and Poles made Catholics a political force in the city. Americans of Protestant stock harbored great fears of these new arrivals and generally regarded their religion as 'foreign and un-American." The newspapers, particularly Medill's and later McCormick's *Tribune* were unreasonably hostile to Catholics (72). Joseph Medill and other prominent Protestant civic leaders formed the American Protective Association, whose members vowed never to vote for or employ Roman Catholics. The APA would be particularly strong at the newly founded University of Chicago. An APA paper called *The Menace had run a slogan: Read* The Menace/Get the Dope/ Go to the polls, and/Put Down the Pope.

Public Schools reinforced a Protestant bias and openly taught Protestant doctrines. As late as 1875 students in Chicago Public schools were required to read from the King James Bible. The American bishops agreed at Baltimore in the 1885, to protect the faith by instituting schools in order to maintain instruction in the faith, while educating the young to be good and productive citizens. The first Catholic schools in Chicago were built by Bishop Quarter and through the next six bishops, as the Catholic population swelled; Catholic parishes dominated the urban landscape. Catholics moved further south, away from the congestion of the River and Back of the Yards and by 1920 the Chicago bungalow which still surrounds Leo High School provided them a home in Auburn.

CARDINAL MUNDELEIN
and
MONSIGNOR
SHEWBRIDGE
at
THE DEDICATION OF
LEO HIGH SCHOOL
IN 1926

Dedication in 1926

II. Leo High School built to serve the young men on Chicago's south side

According to Chicago historian Robert G. Spinncy, the prosperity of the 1920's which provided greater opportunities for working people to purchase homes and some cases automobiles was off-set by a wave of anti-Catholic sentiment which was orchestrated by the Ku Klux Klan. In today's revisionist historical point of view, it is ignored that the Klan directed its hatred at Catholics and Jews as well as African Americans. The perceived threat of Catholic prosperity on so-called 100% America became manifest in the active participation of Chicago businesses in no less than eighteen Klan organizations in the city alone. It is reported that Klan membership in Chicago numbered between 65, 000– 85,000 active members.

This second infestation of the Ku Klux Klan reflected fear of the millions of immigrants, most whom were Catholic in the Midwest. There were cross burnings in front of St. Barnabas, Christ the King, and St. Cajetan parishes in the Beverly Morgan Park neighborhoods. As a result, a greater solidarity and identification with parish burgeoned among Catholics and non-Catholics on the southwest side. Jewish businessmen Bob Klugman, Maurice B. Sachs and Maurice Blackman cultivated a warm and lasting identification with Leo High School. These great men were major patrons of both *The Oriole* and *The Lion*. Mr. Klugman owner of a popular Men's Clothing Shop at 812 W. 79th Street offered a suit of clothing to the leading scorer on the 1938 football eleven. (Vol. X!, # 2. p 3) Mr. Blackman awarded Bulava watches to Leo athletes and Mr. Sachs sponsored scholarships. Bob Hylard of the Class of '47 recalls Jim McKeever '54 saying that in the list of one hundred people who did the most in forming his life Blackman, Klugman, and Sachs are in the top twenty. Simon Blitstein continued this tradition at Mr. Lee's Clothes For Men in the Evergreen Plaza through the 1980's. A graduate of 1968, recalled how his boss, Mr. Si Blitstein, gave him his suit for a homecoming dance, 'take any suit, shirt, and tie – have a nice time, Mick.' These great and generous patrons hired Catholic boys in order to help them pay their tuition. It is no wonder that Leo CISCA members fought anti-Semitic attitudes through their service organization.

Leo High School was a leader in Catholic Action throughout the 1930's, '40's, 50's, and 60's. For God and Country –Pro Deo Et Patria – the cornerstone of Leo High School, commitment and courage is reflected in the service activities of Leo students. CYO meant more than boxing. Bishop Sheil ran half-way houses for newly released convicts, shelters for the homeless, and operated adult education programs long before the New Deal took effect (Kantowicz 189-199). Beginning in 1926, Leo High School had an answer to the Ku Klux Klan and the more subtle bigots who believed that Catholics could not be "100% Americans. "

1953

1953

III. Cardinal Mundelein, Monsignor Shewbridge, & Leo High School.

On Feb. 9^t 1916, George W. Mundelein was installed as Metropolitan Ordinary of Chicago – Archbishop of the West. In September, the Archbishop outlined his plan for Catholic Education. Every parish would have a Catholic school and a place in it for every Catholic child. There would be a uniform curriculum, common textbooks, common transfer card, and common exams. English would be the mandatory medium of instruction. "Our greatest need today is a well-instructed, watchful, active Catholic laity. This is the day and the hour of the layman's apostolate . . . In these days when every appeal is being made to the senses . . . when money, success, and pleasure are the gods of our modern pagan world, then our people need all the old-fashioned Catholic doctrine they can get." From the pulpit and the chalkboard Catholics would receive a uniform instruction in Catholic doctrine.

A Catholic Board of Supervisors was formed to work with religious orders in developing a core curriculum. Catholic education was taking direction from the top though parish pastors would have the responsibility of financing and operating the schools. Like wise, Mundelein had strengthened the concept of the "territorial parish" as distinct from the "ethnic parishes." In most cases the territorial parishes were largely Irish with assimilated Polish, German, Bohemian, Flemish, or Italian parishioners. They were American parishes. The identification culture was Catholic in these territorial parishes.

In 1916, the western territory of St. Leo's Parish was developed into St. Sabina's. More and more families were moving into the former Lake Township. Likewise Mundelein called for the establishment of St. Justin Martyr and St. Dorothy. In Professor Eileen McMahon's *What Parish Are You From*, it is noted that families from the 'ethnic parishes' were also moving to Auburn Gresham. McMahon's intelligent portrait of parish culture in Chicago provides a great study of the people who continue to support Leo High School. They considered themselves Catholic Americans and not Irish or German as such.

Professor McMahon's study should be required reading in all Catholic teacher education programs. It poignantly identifies the core of Catholic culture that lies in the heart of parish. The parish was the center of the lives of the people in the neighborhood and Leo High School was an extension of that identity. The growth of the south side through annexation, the development of infrastructure and housing, and the natural affinity for neighborhood community helped develop Auburn Gresham into a powerful Catholic center of Chicago. However, other Americans were not so fortunate in finding suitable housing. The Black Belt was glutted with new arrivals from the South, but African Americans found little welcome and even less suitable housing.

1918 – America was deeply involved in the Great War; Thousands of citizens enlisted to fight in the war, immigration restrictions were enforced thus crafting a dwindling cheap labor force. Likewise, this shortage of workers led many to demand an increase in wages. American industry replied by hiring African Americans from the South. The Great Migration brought thousands of African Americans from the South to Chicago's south side. The Black population of Chicago rose from 30,000 in 1910 to 80,000 in 1918. In 1920, that number would be swelled by 120,000 new Chicagoans. Most Blacks lived on the thirty block strip along south State Street. Wentworth served as border between Black and white neighborhoods. Many found employment in the Chicago meat packing industry – the number of African American workers in this trade rose from 1,000 in 1905 to 12,000 in 1918.

Blacks sought relief from the Jim Crow South and the promise of higher wages in Chicago, only to be squeezed into the thirty block strip along State Street. Housing for new arrivals was unspeakable to non-existent. The Great Migration to Chicago would impact on and become an integral part of Leo High School's history. In contrast to Chicago's Black Belt, life in Irish Catholic Auburn was characterized by progress into the American social and economic main stream. Parishes often reflected the ethnic make-up of their congregations. In far south side neighborhoods, the Irish and Germans were the dominant groups, demographically, economically, politically, and ecclesiastically.

In 1918 -1919, Chicago was an ethnic powder keg. German Americans were appalled by Woodrow Wilson and the League of Nations' debasement of their homeland, Jews and Poles rioted on Damen and Kedzie Avenues in reaction to anti-Semitic pogroms in Poland, Italy was refused annexation of territories claimed from Austria by Wilson, and the Black population of Chicago doubled during the War. Not only that, a sharp economic recession hit America. Catholics recently discharged from World War I service returned to find many of their former jobs filled by African Americans or recent European arrivals who did not serve in France. Workers struck for fair wages and at one point, 250,000 Chicagoans were out of work. During the war almost no new housing construction took place and tensions between ethnic groups seethed into hatred (Spinney 170).

In 1919 this hatred erupted in a race riot that would leave fifteen whites and twenty-three blacks killed and hundreds of homes burned after six day of horror. Similar riots occurred in Knoxville, Omaha, and Washington D.C. The Chicago riots were by far the worst. They occurred because African Americans posed a challenge to white ethnic Chicagoans for jobs and housing. Not only that, blacks were becoming a powerful political force and this unnerved many whites. African Americans fought back with militancy unheard of in The South they had put behind. The riot was sparked by white bigots who murdered a black boy for swimming on to a 'white only' beach. Blacks, like the Irish, Germans, Poles, Italians, and Jews had had enough. The tensions of 1919 would simmer into our new millennium (Spinney171-172).

However, Rev, Peter Shewbridge went about the work of building a place where courage and commitment would attempt to make a better world. The economy righted itself by the early 1920's. Chicago's steel mills alone accounted for 17% of all the steel produced in America (174). Strikes subsided, unemployment fell, and housing starts kicked in. By 1929, from the Black belt west to the Chicago city limits the Chicago Bungalow covered the southwest side. With this boom, second and third generation Catholics bought single family dwellings and created a need for new parishes. Christ the King, St. Barnabas, St. Cajetan, Little Flower, and many others joined the venerable Nativity, St. Gabriel,

Visitation, Sacred Heart, St. Martin De Pores, St. John of God, St. Brendan's, St. Basil, St. Sabina and St. Leo the Great parishes. Toward Lake Michigan, St. Philip Neri and Our Lady of Peace served the affluent Catholics of Chicago's south shore. By 1920, Rev. Shewbridge was financially solvent enough to petition Cardinal Mundelein for a boy's high school that would serve as a Central school for mushrooming Catholic population. Archbishop Mundelein (elevated to the Cardinalate in 1924) shared Shewbridge's enthusiasm for education (Martin 91-92).

With so many parishes growing in population the need for a central Catholic school for boys in Auburn became apparent. Ordained to the priesthood in 1896, Peter F. Shewbridge, a Chicago native and energetic young pastor put necessity into action. The families in Auburn were comfortable but certainly not affluent. Costs of Living were formalized for the first time with the establishment of the Consumer Price Index in 1918, in response to war production and employment. The birth rate among parishioners was astounding according to the baptismal records in Prof. Eileen McMahon's study of south side parishes *What Parish Are you From?* As Catholic families moved close to the American middle class many wanted their children to prepare for appropriate careers and maintain Catholic instruction.

Father Shewbridge wanted a high school for boys that would have St. Leo Parish as its center. Leo High School would prepare young men for higher education and also provide opportunities to compete for clerical and financial careers. The Catholic population in Auburn grew dramatically through the 1890's and by 1901 the original St. Leo's was replaced with a larger more beautiful Lombardy-style edifice. St. Leo parish briefly operated a high school for girls as well as its grammar school. Flat buildings and brick bungalows sprouted

17

among the older wooden frame structures, reflective of the area's semi-rural past. The south side became one of the largest Irish Catholic regions in the world.

Archbishop George William Mundelein, "a fierce Americanizer," though a German American, was appointed in 1916 (Martin 129). The native New Yorker was an academic prodigy who caught the attention of President Grover Cleveland who offered the young Catholic an appointment to the U.S. Naval Academy. However, the pious young man was determined to devote his life to the Church. He applied to the Diocese of Brooklyn and won the sponsorship of Bishop McDonnell who sent the young seminarian to Rome for his studies. Mundelein was ordained a priest in 1895, appointed Chancellor of the Brooklyn Diocese in 1897, and elevated to Episcopal rank in 1909. He proved an astute business manager and a powerful patron of Catholic schools (Martin 66).

It was Mundelein's intention to end the ethnocentrism in the Chicago parishes. Likewise, Mundelein sought to mainstream Catholics into American society through education. He also firmly held that Catholic schools should promote vocations in order that the ranks of religious would be filled by well-educated individuals. Mundelein pushed the concept of the central Catholic high school, as the means of educating young people to be good productive citizens as well as good Catholics. Instruction in English was mandated for all disciplines in Catholic schools. Catholic schools in Chicago would reflect devotion to God and Country.

> "We Catholics occupy a unique position with regard to our schools. We do not criticize and decry the public school system as all wrong. We simply say it is not enough for us. The State school system educates the mind, the intellect, but it neglects the heart, the moral, the spiritual part of man, and that means the

18

principal, the most necessary part of him. We maintain that to educate the mind and neglect the soul is an experiment that is fraught with danger to the individual and to the State as well. Buts as we do not seek to force our views on others, we build and maintain our own schools, at our own expense, while bearing our burden of the State schools as well. And, as we are people of very moderate means, we feel that we are indeed giving a splendid example of devotion to our religion and love of our country, too" (martin)

Leo High School was designed by Joseph W. McCarthy a student of the great Daniel Burnham – like Mundelein a man who made no small plans. McCarthy had also designed all of the buildings on the magnificent St. Mary of the Lake campus in Mundelein.

The actual corner-stone blessed by Mundelein at the dedication of Leo High School on September 7, 1926 is inscribed Pro Deo et Patria – for God and Country. As much a part of St. Leo Parish and Pastor Shewbridge's vision, so it is George Cardinal Mundelein's. (Insert 7 Educational Objectives of LHS) Mundelein would become an energetic force in advancing American values and patriotism through education. Though Pastor Shewbridge's flock would be largely Irish, the high school that would serve them would promote an American Catholicism. The parishioners while by no means affluent prospered in boom years of the 1920's.

The prosperity of the 1920's was also made remarkable by the Prohibition Amendment of 1919. What began as a 'holy' alliance of social reformers and anti-immigrant bigots gave birth to the criminal gangs with the financial muscle to control politicians. The *de facto* Mayor of Chicago was Al Capone while William Hale (Big Bill) Thompson held the Office *de jure*. Most Chicagoans were undisturbed by the gang violence of the late 1920's and early '30's. More than a few men buried at Mount

Olivet and Holy Sepulcher had rosaries wrapped around their gun hands.

Auburn Highlands home to Leo High School was the domain of the Spike O'Donnell gang (headquartered in the Highland Theatre Building at 79ᵗʰ & Ashland) which controlled breweries and speakeasies. Like the Gangster Disciples and Stones who traffic in drugs today, fast money was a lure to tough young guys through illegal sales of liquor. Gangsters like Frank McErlean, George Bucher, George Meehan, Ralph Sheldon, and Tommy Hoban littered the streets with their victims while Father Shewbridge planned a central Catholic high school that would be a haven for boys who wanted to succeed. Frank McErlean, topped off with whiskey, Tommy gunned anything visible at 78ᵗʰ & Crandon on a September night in 1931. That same evening Leo High School senior Thomas A. Murphy was no doubt doing his homework. McErlean would drink himself to death in Beardstown, IL the next year. Thomas Murphy would graduate from Leo go on to University of Illinois and become the Chairman of the Board of General Motors. McErlean is buried at Holy Sepulcher and Murphy continues to send thousands of dollars back to Leo High School.

Issues like an education for their children and paying the mortgage on the flat building or bungalow dominated most people's thoughts. Getting a fair wage and decent hours and work conditions were great concerns. At the turn of this century we are insulated by a quality of life that has the American labor movement to thank. Issues like safety in the work place, the right to collective bargaining, overtime, and health and welfare were struggled and bled for by working people in the last century. The labor movement was an important vehicle for most people in the stride toward middle class living. In fact Leo High School would not take the name of the Pope who saved Rome from the Huns, but for the Pope of the Workingman – Leo XIII. Pope Leo XIII's Encyclical

Rerum Novarum was a defense of the rights of workers to organize and demand fair wages and working conditions.

While most Catholics were pro-labor, they were also fiercely anti-Communist. The American Lefties lined up with those who executed priests and nuns in Spain and thought Joe Stalin to be a great old guy. To American Catholics of the early days of Leo, Hitler, Stalin, Mussolini, and Tojo were comparable to manure in its many manifestations – deeds not words constituted evil. As most people in St. Leo's Parish were blue-collar people and many actively involved in the labor movement, the choice of name was fitting – Leo High School – in honor of the working man's Pope. The sacrifices made by members of organized labor gave America the standard of living that it now takes for granted.

Working people were paying the bills and former parishioners who had some money reached back and contributed to the new school. The nouveau riche Catholics remembered their roots. It was pretty tough for E. Austin Duffy, Esq. of the law firm of Sycholm, Squeesome, and Bylholm to forget that he was' Eddie Duffy from the Tile Yards on Lowe –who put cardboard in his brogans – and ate bread and lard sandwiches.' Many boys who brought home coal from along the train tracks developed into tough legal in-fighters, who would get snatched up by the blue stocking law firms.

Justice Thomas Fitzgerald carried a union card most of his life and graced the bench of Cook County's Circuit Court Criminal Division with his integrity and courage. Now an Illinois Supreme Court Justice, "Fitz" protects Illinois citizens as the State Constitution's custodian. Like Judge Richard Curry, Justice Fitzgerald remembers his roots. Chicago's current legal pit bulls like Frank Coglianese, Joe Power, Mike Kelly, Dan Fusco, Tom Durkin, Bill Conlan, Jim Collins, and Bob Joyce combine

21

street smart tenacity and Catholic core values. Joe Power ('70), who was tutored in reading by Brother Pete Doyle, brought down Illinois Governor George Ryan by doggedly fighting for the justice denied to the Willis family. The late great Eddie Proctor '47, who had been the go-to-guy for the Archdiocese of Chicago and a leading real estate law professor at Loyola university, helped Leo without fee all through his heroic battle with cancer. Tom Durkin defends the neediest defendants –those whom the public has already judged to be guilty: Matt Hale the racist 'church' leader and people accused of aiding the Hamas. Tom teaches a Constitutional Law Seminar to Leo Seniors – Pro Bono.

Leo would become the proving grounds for future labor leaders, pro-labor legislators, activist judges, and labor lawyers like Martin Burns '45, J. Dillon Hoey'59 and Jay Luchsinger '68. Hundreds of more Leo men would become active in the trades unions. Leo High School reflected the values of labor – the courage to demand fair wages and dignified conditions and the commitment to ensure that one did not cross certain lines. Union contractors like John Hopkins '69, Tom Hopkins '73, Mike Regan '70 work to maintain the dignity of the worker. Denny Sexton '65 leads Carpenters Local 13. Illinois State Senator Ed Maloney '66 and State Representative Kevin McCarthy '68 have strong ties to labor. Tom Keaty '73 is a Trustee of Engineers Local # 399.

Catholic workers remembered that the Body of Christ is the ultimate union. The Church and parish continued to be the centering influence of Catholic life. The Depression affected everyone and the parish made sure that every young man who wanted a Leo education would find a place here. That tradition is still very much in place at Leo High School. St. George, St. Phillip, St. Rita, Mount Carmel, and DeLaSalle took the same attitude towards their constituents. Everyone reached out to help their neighbors.

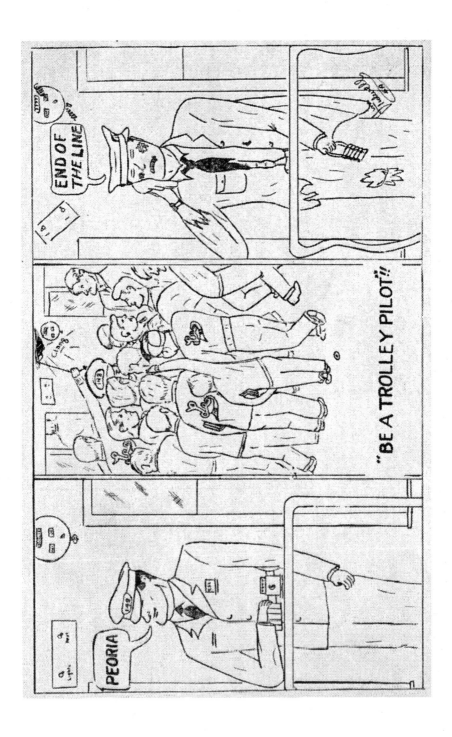

Shawbridge Stadium, the realization of Monsignor Shawbridge's dreams, served as the home of the 1947 Catholic League Champs.

REV. BR. T. P. TREACY
Assistant Athletic Director

REV. BROTHER FRANCIS R. FINCH
Athletic Director

Football
1947

Here's How We Got There

FRANK JENKS
Assistant Coach

JOSEPH "RED" GLEASON
Head Coach

Football
1947

Frank McGuire gets advice from the Leo coaching staff: Mr. Jenks, Mr. Gleason, and Mr. William Bambrick.

IV.   The Christian Brothers of Ireland – The Roots of Leo's History

The positive values of the parish at large could be summed up in the lives of Religious men and women who taught in Catholic schools. The Irish Christian Brothers were men who sacrificed their talents and skills without any thought of financial remuneration, the possibility of enjoying the comforts of a wife and family, and the balm of recognition for accomplishments. The Brothers lived in great simplicity in cramped apartments first on Peoria Street and later on Sangamon Street. Finally in 1950, a monastery building was completed to house the Brothers of Leo. Their devotion to the young men that they served is best summed up in the life Brother Francis Rupert Finch. One Brother who transcended the history of Leo Francis Rupert Finch seems to embody the very essence of Blessed Edmund Rice's mission for his congregation of Brothers. Beginning in the early 1930's and only interrupted by teaching duties and congregation obligations for a few years, Brother Finch touched the lives Leo men in every decade. He will be the focus of a chapter to come.

Francis Rupert Finch is the finest example of the Brothers who molded Leo men. An orphan, born in St. Louis and raised in a home run by the Christian Brothers of Ireland, young Francis Finch became a great scholar and athlete. Most of his career was devoted to the students of Leo High School. In his last years at Leo, Brother Finch amazed the young men that he taught Chemistry, Algebra, and Physics.

A Christmas anecdote From *the Oriole, 1947:* concerning Bro. Finch tells of an exam paper handed him by a student with the comment: "God alone knows the answer to this question, Merry Christmas"

> Never the one to be outdone by a mere broth of a boy, Br. Returned the exam with this cheery notation: "God gets an A; you get an F. Happy New Year."

Lastly, Brother Patrick D. McCormick, the last Irish Christian Brother to serve as principal of Leo High School, and himself a singular champion of Leo High School during its most difficult time in the late 1980's offers a poignant portrait of this saint in our midst:

Discipline was the *sine qua non* in Catholic education. The Brothers had a reputation for getting gallons of metaphorical blood from their adolescent turnips. Bro. Pakenham once admonished two seniors caught in the act of something, 'I thought I heard horseplay, but then I noticed your ears." However, much of the contemporary mythology concerning the disciplinary methods of the Brothers seems to have had its roots some time late in the school's history. The great affection for early brothers is very evident from Leo men dating to the Charter and through the 1940's. This is reflected admirably in the surviving pages of *The Oriole* and *The Lion*. Not only that, it must be noted that so many Leo men followed the path of their teachers. It has been said that at one time Leo High School had the greatest number of graduates in Holy Orders. The vocations were generated by the example of the complex men who occupied the flat building on Peoria Street. The Irish Christian Brothers followed the triple vows of Poverty, Chastity, and Obedience. One of Chicago's outstanding Churchmen is Bishop John Gorman '43, who recently established the Bishop Gorman School of Institutional Advancement at St. Xavier University, Father William Joseph McFarlane '83, a son of St. Gabe's in Canaryville, who ran as a "Republican" for Alderman of the 11th Ward and another is Father John Sullivan '68, Chaplain for the Illinois Police Association. These men heard the call of Christ while at Leo.

The academic credentials of the Christian Brothers who staffed Leo High School through the 1930'-40's are astounding. Many had been athletes in Ireland and quite a few had reputations as boxers. Brother King had been a champion boxer in Canada. Brother "Moose" Haley patrolled the East end of the third floor and would invite "malefactors" into his classroom for a personal remonstrance, but he was the only faculty member invited to the Class of 1946 Silver Anniversary. Kindly Brother Daly assessed library overdue fines only when there was a movie playing at the Capitol on Halsted that he particularly wanted to see. The deep affection for this man is evident in the pages of *The Oriel:* in WWII Leo men on furlough used some of that precious time to visit Brother Daly.

These remarkably talented men lived in strict poverty and with great humility followed the directions of their superiors. Their lives were truly dedicated to Christ and to the mission of their Congregation. Their example kindled the warmth of Faith in the young men they instructed and each year Leo High School could boast of new vocations.

This could not have happened without a genuine commitment on their part to the life of strenuous service that was witnessed by hundreds of tough teenage boys. No cynical wolves in sheep's' clothing could have directed so many young men to take up a life of Poverty, Chastity, and Obedience.   In 1938, The Oriole reported that –

> James J. Doherty of 5733 Sangamon Street was ordained to the priesthood by Cardinal Mundelein on April 15th. Father Doherty is a member of the Class of 1931 and the first Leo graduate to be ordained a priest. . . . . As a tribute to his old school Father Doherty celebrated Mass in the School chapel in the presence of the Faculty and entire Student body on Thursday, May 11. (Vol. XI. No.6. page One).

In the same issue two graduates Eugene Pilon ('31) and Robert Scanlon ('30) took vows of profession in the Congregation of Christian Brothers of Ireland.   There is powerful evidence that the values of home and parish were so strongly reinforced by the Brothers that Leo graduates would spread Christ's work to the broader world.   The call of Pope Pius XI for Catholic Action took root in the consciences of Chicago's Catholics. Between 1916 and 1934 eighty-six new parishes were organized, sixty-eight new grammar schools, thirty-one high schools (17 boys, 14 girls) built. By the count of the Archdiocese of Chicago, more than six hundred buildings ministering to Roman Catholics could be accounted its property. Each structure was built during the administration of Archbishop Mundelein.

Along with instruction in religion, Leo men were encouraged to participate in The Sodality of Our Lady, The League of the Sacred Heart, CISCA, and all students were enrolled in the Knights of the Blessed Sacrament. Diocesan priests particularly men like Father Bill Murphy

(a St. Rita Alumnus no less) spent many hours at Leo High School giving counsel, hearing confessions, and ministering to the young men in general. There is not yearbook through the 1950's that does not have a snap-shot of Father Murphy attending sports events, banquets, and concerts. In 2004, Father Murphy makes sure that every Leo gathering is on his calendar. That includes membership in the Nellie Fox Society which was founded by Leo men E. Michael Kelly '65, and Illinois Supreme Court Justice Thomas Fitzgerald '59.

Chicago Fire Commissioner James T. Joyce (Leo '60) addressed the Nellie Fox Society on the occasion of Nellie Fox's induction into the Baseball Hall of Fame in 2000 and informed the uninitiated to Leoite apocrypha by informing the crowd that Leo's school newspaper *The Oriole* was the only high school journal with its own obituary column and that the library's only caveat was 'don't bleed on the books.' These light-hearted counter punches reflected the more physical nature of school discipline in the 1950's.   Bill Nelligan '60 added to his manly aura as a freshman. He was clouted no less than five times before lunch on his first day at Leo High School. Leo men have catalogues of yarns detailing the litany of punishments meted out. The cherry on the sundae follows:

In the very late 1950's a Leo student was named Catholic Teenager of the Year.   This honor was bestowed in Washington, D.C. and broadcast on the national television with Bishop Fulton J. Sheen making the presentation. The female recipient was Annette Funicello – the busty Mousketeer of the Walt Disney Empire. The Leo Man filled his eyes with Ms Funicello' bounteous proportions – on camera. Upon his return to school, the conquering hero was cold cocked by Brother Sloan. 'The next time you get an award – mind

29

them eyes!' It is tough to develop a powerful ego on the south side of Chicago.

Bill Nelson '50 remarked that giving money to Leo High School while the Christian Brothers operated the school was like "having the recently paroled from Joliet Penitentiary taking up a collection for their former guards." Due to the growth of the school population in the late '40s through the 50's, discipline seems to have taken on a more corporeal aspect, than in the 30's and 40's. The school that had been planned for 800 students swelled to over 1,500 by the 1950's. Discipline of these tough, head strong and proud young men was difficult enough but the near double the labor must have contributed to the strain on the teachers. The litany of stories about clouts and knocks from the brothers nevertheless betrays a spirit of mutual affection. Tough guys, after all, can and do take it.

Brothers like the legendary Bros. Doorley, Curtis, Ryan, Birmingham, J.S. O'Keefe and the saintly Brother Finch were men truly dedicated to Christ's command to go and teach. Leo produced many great scholars who would honor its name in academia. Larry McCaffrey ('43) after serving in the Coast Guard in WWII would become the Distinguished Professor of History at Loyola University of Chicago and the author of many books and articles on American and Irish history. Professor McCaffrey continues to lecture at the Newbury Library. The Brothers and their lay counterparts served their students well, lay teachers got their licks in as well as the Brothers. The kindly Brother Daly is remembered to have fostered a love of learning through books and music. His library was a scholarly sanctuary respected by scholars and hoods alike.

Most Brothers are remembered with great affection and gratitude, like Brothers Finch, Collins, Birmingham, Coogan, and O'Keefe. However, a clout on the noggin or a slap with the strap had its place in the curriculum. To put things into context the Brothers were confronted with male teenagers and these were tough, tough young men. Their parents were tough people. Toughness is too often mistaken for cruelty.

Rather, these parishioners could take it. First, they leave their native homes, they work in demanding and exhausting conditions for which they receive small compensation, they endure hardship, but they sacrifice to build churches and schools for future generations. They all believe that their neighbor has it much harder than they do themselves. These were very tough people. Case in point: General Thomas P. Gerrity '30.

General Gerrity was a member of the 3rd Bomb Group in World War II. On December 8th 1941, he was ordered to bomb a reported Japanese invasion fleet off of Luzon in the Philippines. His orders came through too late. As he prepared to take off from Nichols Field his obsolete B-18 was strafed and bombed. One of Gerrity's hands was injured in the attack. Gerrity was re-assigned to a fighter squadron on Bataan, from January through March they battled the Japanese until all of their planes were disabled. As a result, he was assigned to ground duties on Bataan.

The story of Bataan is an American legend. Americans and Filipinos fought a heroic holding action and stalled the Japanese conquest of the Pacific for four months. They bought time for America with their lives. In April, 1942, the final days before the fall of Bataan, Gerrity and a few of his fellow pilots were asked to volunteer for an attempt to escape to Australia, where America had more planes than pilots. Gerrity and his companions restored a shot up amphibious plane and began what amounted to a suicide journey of thousands of miles.

31

They flew the entire length of the Philippine Archipelago, dodging Japanese planes and ships, refueling where they could. They arrived at the last American airfield on the island of Mindanao, where an Army plane picked them up for the final leg to Australia.

In Australia, Tom Gerrity (down to 96 lbs from 156 lbs) recuperated. Gerrity spent the next year sinking 28 Japanese warships from his B-25, and was one of the originators of the skip-bombing tactic. He would go on to become a four star general and overall commander of American Bomber forces. The U.S. Air Force named one of its highest awards for General Gerrity – Leo '30.

Tom Gerrity graduated from Leo and like many of his schoolmates went into engineering at the Armour Institute which is now Illinois Institute of Illinois. Leo graduates had the aptitude and tenacity to become successful. Leo Alumni continue to support young men who want to succeed. The fields of architecture, design and engineering have been honored by the work of Leo men.

Patrick Daly '67 is a leading Chicago architect and a Board member of IIT. John Q. O'Donnell '68 is the Chief Financial Officer of the John Buck Company –the most prominent real estate development company in Chicago. Gen. (ret.) George Muellner '61, like General Gerrity a combat pilot with more than 600 combat missions in Vietnam, developed the STAR program (Gen. Muellner is featured frequently on the History Channel) used in both Gulf Wars and is now the President of Boeing Corporations Strategic Weapons, Satellites, and Space Division. Dr. Thomas Reidy developed the polygraph test. Harry Richards went on to Rochester Institute of Technology and formed his own Graphics Design Corporation. Dick Landis CEO of Landis Plastics makes the containers from which you folks spoon your yogurt. Likewise, the litany of accounting and business leaders who competed for placement at America's greatest colleges and universities is staggering. A listing of all Leo Alumni and their fields of endeavor will follow. Deane Thomas '47 went on to Northwestern University. Bill Koloseike '48 a stand-out athlete and student and Gerry Haggerty '54 have gone to become the largest automobile dealers in the Chicago area. Bill Kay is a top sponsor of this great school and Gerry Haggerty is in the front of the line when help is needed. Both men are Leo Hall of Fame inductees. The values of the Parish reinforced at Leo High School in no small way sparked the drive in these great men.

1952

V.   The Depression Era Values & Militant Catholicism: CISCA, & Athletics

In 1918, St. Leo's and St. Sabina's were two of the largest parishes on the south side. Both parishes were represented by a mix of middle class and working class families. Many heads of household stayed home to take care of the kids, while the Dad's labored in the trades, drove streetcars, served as policemen and firemen, or clerked for the Stockyards or at offices in the Loop.

In 1918, Pastor Shewbridge was assigned to the Romanesque Church at 78th & Emerald, after having founded St. Gertrude's Parish in Glenwood, IL. This energetic young priest was chosen to shepherd the rapidly growing parish of St. Leo's. The boundaries for the parish were set by the Archdiocese: roughly 72nd street on the north to 83rd St. south and from State Street to Carpenter east to west. Parish boundaries may have shifted slightly through the 40's and 50's with St. Sabina's Parish.

On Monday, September 28th, 1925, the Archdiocesan Consulters granted permission for Father Shewbridge to apply $ 525,000 to complete the building of a school to serve 800 boys with the capability to expand capacity to 1,300. Auxiliary Bishop Hoban informed Shewbridge that he could purchase a seven acre property at 74th & Aberdeen for $ 125,000 in 1927.   Likewise, Christian Brothers of Ireland from New York received permission from Archbishop Mundelein to come to Chicago and operate the new central high school they were given an apartment building on Peoria Street which would serve as a temporary residence and the deed to the building was given to the congregation. Four Brothers established the first monastery of Irish Christian Brothers in the Midwest – Brothers Doorley, Grange, O'Donnell, and Filehne. Brother Doorley was Leo High School's first Principal. These men were the first Irish Christian Brothers in Chicago.

The doors opened on September 9, 1926 to 122 young men from south side parishes. The majority would come from St. Leo and St. Sabina's parishes but many others traveled great distances to be educated in this new central high school. Thomas Parsons of Blue Island, Illinois would travel the ten miles by many streetcars for his Leo Education. Most of the travel was through unincorporated townships and Tom had to run between stops; sometimes a mile at a time. The payoff was worth the effort. Still others journeyed from the steel mills of Chicago's south east side and came from Croatian, Polish, and Italian parishes.   Four Brothers and one hundred twenty-two registered freshmen were a great start to a great school.

In 1927, Leo took home its first trophy defeating St. George High School 21-0 in football.   Behind the leadership of Mr. Ike Mahoney, a star player at Creighton University and the Chicago Cardinals, the Leo High School "Fighting Irish" made history. Playing a freshman schedule that included Aquinas High School, Morgan Park Military Academy, Morgan Park High School,

Downers Grove High School, and DeLaSalle Academy of Joliet, Mahoney's Irish gelled into a powerful force. Shortly before entering the Catholic League Leo High School adopted the name of the Lions –in deference to the men from other backgrounds and in keeping with the name of the school. The Lions throated a roar still echoing today. The early Leo teams impressed the Chicago newspapers and received headline sports treatment for individuals like the quarterback who would become the Assistant United States Secretary of Commerce Robert Podesta. Along with names like Maher, Doyle, O'Connor, Ryan, Hamill, Kennedy, Kelly, and Lavin, were Leo men Mortensen, Ganka, Nuber, and Reker. Nello Sabatini, owner of Franconello's Restaurant and a prominent Chicago political operative noted that he was badly treated by the Irish at Leo. Tom Mahoney '53 & Bill Nelligan '60 agreed - the Irish were rotten to them as well.

In *The Oriole, Feb. 14, 1947.* A feature writer slyly implied some ethnic favoritism when announcing the names of the two students with highest semester averages:

> Tops in the school was 4A's pride and joy Joe McNitt. He breezed through the ordeal (semester grade reports) with a paltry 97.3 average. It must get to be a habit for Joe's been on that honor list since 1B saw his exalted presence, and that's quite awhile. I have trouble remembering that far back.

> Among the juniors, that distinguished president of the distinguished 3A class topped all his classmates with a smashing 96.6. His name is Dennis O'Brien. (Did you ever notice that we're taught by Irish Christian Brothers . Then notice who tops the honor roll. O'Brien and Mc Nitt. I should have gone to Weber).

The author betrays his ethnic origins by referring to a proudly Polish Catholic high school on the north side but never prints his name. It is refreshingly evident that at least two sons of Erin possess a capacity for academics. Dennis O'Brien '48 became the President of Rochester University in New York and the author of many books and articles Professor George "Denny" O'Brien was inducted into the Leo Hall of Fame in 2004. Joe McNitt '47 went on to University of Notre Dame and Northwestern Law School. Guys with czy's, vich's, and vowel ending names made pretty good academic records at Leo High School. Andy Placco'45 won a full scholarship to University of Chicago. Bob Podesta '30 went on to Northwestern, John Frederick Nimmsof '31 a Notre Dame graduate distinguished himself as a lecturer and poet teaching at Yale, Princeton, and University of Chicago. Pretty good ethnically balanced record for some south side boys.

They shared the Faith of their fathers and committed their energies to live up to the expectations of their parishes for them. These young men witnessed the sacrifices their families made in providing them with an education. Dad's shoes and Mom's clothes boiler took a back seat to young Dinny's tuition. Second and third jobs for the breadwinners were not unheard of in this community. Likewise, the Parish was not ignored in the earner's mathematics. Standing inside of St. Margaret of Scotland at 97th & Throop, one can get a feel for the devotion of the people who built out of love of God. It was not enough to have an enclosed space for a meeting. Only an ambience that reflected the impact of God's love for his people would do. Families would pool resources to purchase stained glass, statuary, altars, tabernacles, pews, and in many Churches like St. Margaret of Scotland, majestic oratories. These people were part of a dynamic Christianity - it was orthodox but anything but static. The Churches were filled and the pastors and their curates had more than their share of work.

The operation of Leo High School in 1929/30 as reflected in the North Central Association of Colleges and Secondary Schools report by Brothers Curtis and Doorley was conducted by Pastor Shewbridge, seventeen Irish Christian Brothers, and four laymen: J.J. Miles, C. Reinke, E.A. Dwyer, and F.J."Ike" Mahoney. All four laymen in this Charter year of 1929/30 received combined compensation packages amounting to $ 8,400.

In that Charter year, there were 520 students. The building, constructed in 1926 at a total cost of $1,000,000, had a capacity for 800 students. The former Molloy Field was purchased at a total cost of $ 200,000 and added 7 acres to the campus. The school day extended from 9:00 A.M. until 3:00 P.M. and featured a rigorous course of study that included Latin, French, Spanish, Algebra, Math, Trigonometry, Chemistry, Physics, Natural Science, Civics, Geography, History, and Commercial studies. Religious instruction filled out the schedule and was the focusing mechanism of all studies. There was a great emphasis on public speaking and students were asked to do recitations on numerous occasions. Instruction was serious and attention was demanded. The deed doers of Leo High School dominated the sports pages of the 1930's & 40's but they also won laurels for academics and forensics. The Leo Band evolved into an orchestra and Glee Club which would make recordings and broadcasts well beyond the Chicago area.

Catholic parishes participated in Catholic Youth Organization (CYO) sponsored programs. Auxiliary Bishop Bernard Sheil who directed CYO implemented a three pronged trident of focus for this program: Intellectual, Spiritual, and Physical. Bishop Sheil has been given short shrift by the Church he championed. It seems that the more intellectually chic Jocist movement, sparked by the charismatic Monsignor Reynold Hillenbrand, clouded the achievements of the earthy and dynamic

Bishop Sheil. His Catholicism was much too "muscular." Nevertheless, it can be argued that Sheil's tactile charity appealed to many more Catholics than the cerebral Hillenbrand's disciples.

Upon the death of Cardinal Mundelein, Bishop Sheil, at least to this Catholic, was treated shabbily by the Chicago Church. But Catholic parishioners remember the great work of Bishop Sheil. Catholic parishioners encouraged their children to compete in study clubs, attend retreats, and join athletic teams – this was "active" Catholic Action. One could see results. CYO provided scholarship opportunities for families hit hard by the Depression.

In 1934, 200,000 Chicagoans participated in CYO programs. These parish level programs helped give young people a leg up toward high school and beyond. Many Leo scholars and athletes earned their spurs through the CYO. The Boy Scouts of America had required membership in sponsoring Protestant churches. Archbishop Mundelein organized a Catholic division of Scouting in 1930. Catholic scouts would follow the regular Boy Scout program but attend an annual retreat at St. Mary of the Lake. The parish remained the focus of all activities.

As such Leo High School maintained the importance of parish identity within the traditions of the school itself. The freshman class of 1939 represented eighty - six south side parishes. The very powerful loyalty to parish merged into an expansive pride in Leo High School. Italians, Germans, Poles, Lithuanians, and Irish blended into Leoites who shared their talents in order to advance the reputation of the school. By extension the Leo men were moving out into the world through Chicago Interscholastic Catholic Action(CISCA), Knights of the Blessed Sacrament (KBS,) Debate, Theatre, Glee Club, Band & orchestra, as well as athletics. Jim Sheridan

'42 broadcast his award winning exclamatory essay – *Making of the U.S. Constitution over WGN radio.*

Leo High School continued the tradition of strong parish identification of its students through the 1980's. By the 1990's two factors emerged that would diminish the Catholic parish identities at Leo – the number of Catholic students became dramatically diminished and The Archdiocese of Chicago began to close parishes and schools in the inner city.

Leo High School like other Catholic high schools was a reflection of the people who established them. While there is intense rivalry and competition among the Catholic High Schools, there is a far deeper mutual respect and affection. Mount Carmel, St. Rita, Fenwick, Loyola, and all of the other Catholic schools get cheers for the continued success of one another. We are the same; but if you want to get a (fill in any rival Catholic League school) graduate off of your front porch – pay for the pizza!

The academic, athletic, social, and religious traditions helped breed a consciousness that is powerfully evident today. Leo High School is like no other in the fact that white Catholic patrons of the school have no tangible stake in continuing a legacy of family names, as they do at St. Rita, Mount Carmel, and DeLaSalle Institute. The great grandchildren of Leo Alumni do not attend Leo High School. In 2003, no Leo student is the son of a Leo graduate. African American graduates of Leo high School will make significant contributions to this school. What must be taken into account is the fact that Leo High School is supported by its Alumni and the level and intensity of the financial support must be bolstered by African American Alumni as they take their places in the corporate, political, and cultural world.

The Catholic values reflected in Leo's history are the motivating factor of support. The impact of the Leo experience requires Alumni support. Those who have experienced Leo High School have absorbed the spirit that moves it forward, regardless of the faith an individual follows. The values of parish so evidently nurtured at Leo High School explain this phenomenon. The individual is great because he is a participant in something greater than himself. Like the magnificent Catholic churches that continue to dominate the Chicago landscape, the spirit of Leo High School evolved as a composition of goodwill past and present. The active collaboration between parents, students, teachers, coaches, and alumni have had and continues to have a positive impact on the larger world.

Michael Thompson '72 is President of a corporation in Wisconsin, after having worked in McDonald's Corporation as International Sales Representative. Andrew Mc Kenna '47 CEO of Schwarz Paper is on the Board of Directors of Mc Donald's Corporation. Both men have their roots in the Leo experience. Michael Thompson played on the legendary 1972/73 (15-2) Catholic League Championship Team with Tony Parker, Jerry Newell, Jim McEldowney , Ron Simmons, Jeffrey Jones, and under Coach of the Year Tom O'Malley.(O'Malley's basketball team is legendary for having the honor of being the only team Hirsch High School refused to play.) After taking a bachelors degree at Cornell University, Michael Thompson began a corporate career in the food industry which continues as President of Fair Oaks Farms Products. Andy McKenna '47 was the Oriole Sports Editor succeeding Bob Hylard '46, as the *Lion's Lair* writer. On to Notre Dame and DePaul Law, McKenna began a career with Schwarz Paper Company in Michigan City, IN. His love of sports lead McKenna to invest in a Michigan City farm team and later as an owner of the Chicago White Sox with Roland Hemond.

Taking Schwarz Paper to the top of the packaging industry, Andy McKenna found himself serving on many corporate, civic, religious and charitable boards of directors. Most importantly, along with Frank Considine '38, Andy McKenna provides Leo High School with frank and accurate opinions on strategic planning. The man answers his own phone for the love of God!

In 1970, Anwar Sadat invited three prominent American business leaders to Cairo following the death of Gamal Nasser to help westernize the Egyptian commerce after so many years of Soviet influence. Thomas A. Murphy Leo '33 CEO General Motors, Frank Considine '37, CEO American National Can and President of the Egypt Business Relations Team, and Robert Podesta Asst. Secretary of Commerce '30 stood on the roof of their hotel overlooking the Nile -- One of them remarked 'imagine, three kids from Leo High School standing at sunset on a roof overlooking the Nile!' Imagine indeed.

Imagine seeing a gun pulled and being directed at the man most responsible for the entire nation. Unflinching, Secret Service Agent Tim McCarthy '67 dove spread-eagle into the path of the shot intended for the President, taking a Devastator bullet in the abdomen. To this day, Mrs. Nancy Reagan calls McCarthy the man who saved her husband. Some mopes think that Hinckley should be allowed greater privileges. I'm sure Hinckley's targets could have done without his love notes to Jodie Foster. The intrusive narrator takes liberties, but I digress.

The Irish Christian Brothers established Leo High School's powerful reputation for scholarship, citizenship, and sportsmanship. From their modest residence on Peoria, the Brothers brought to Leo a powerful sense of purpose that must be applied in every endeavor. This' message

43

received' is evident in the regular start of school edition of *The Oriole: Welcome Freshman:*

> It has been the aim of the freshman class to equal or excel (sic) the record set by its predecessors. You of 1938 must keep up the high standards set by them who have gone before you. The present sophomore classes hands down to you the torch of success. It remains for you to keep its flame alight. Whether you succeed or fail in your attempt may be determined by your attitude toward your school, your studies, and your fellow students.
>
> A tradition has been set up at Leo of keeping your school ever to the fore. You can uphold and enhance it by good work in your studies, becoming imbued with the school spirit and supporting its various activities.
>
> We do not feel this is asking too much of you. Without a doubt, you heard of Leo's standard long before you decided to become a member of its student body. We therefore believe that you should not feel it a burden when we ask you to try your best to uphold the good name of Leo even though it takes a bit more effort on your part than you have been accustomed to put forth. (VOL. XI, No. 1. page 2).

"Even though its takes a bit more effort on your part than you has been accustomed to put forth – "the very assumption that Leo would demand more of the young men who entered this school signals the message received from those charged with their education. There is a mutual respect evident in the pages of *The Oriole* from 1938 through 1947 that jumps out at the reader. The Brothers are held in such high esteem for their scholarship and their Christianity.

Brothers are quoted in the humor columns, the editorials, the sport news, and featured with great respect in the student cartoons. There is no lampooning nor is there evidence of any unhappiness on the part of students. A powerful pride is evident.

There is also a great deal of parish pride and chest thumping. The Parish grammar schools are regularly treated to high praise for student achievement at Leo High School. A regular feature of the student paper is the Honor Roll Lists that reflect friendly competition between the parishes for the total number of Honors men. St. Sabina and St. Leo battle as much for academic bragging rights as did the Lions with Mt. Carmel, or St. Rita in athletics. I remember when Jim Strom '63 received the Leo Mothers Club Gold Medal for English – the nuns at Little Flower Grammar School pounced on most of the credit: 'after all, Jim was prepared by us, don't you know?" Jim, a National Merit Scholar and National Honors Society member, had small part in the Honor. We won't mention the fact that Jack Gaynor '63 of St. John the Baptist took top honors – Lord save us!

Like the Brothers, the laymen who served in the early years were dedicated gentlemen. Their salary compensation reflected in the Annual reports to North Central is humbling. Leo alumni remember the many kindnesses extended to them by the lay teachers. Every Leo student was enlisted in the Knights of the Blessed Sacrament. The Chicago Inter Scholastic Catholic Action (C.I.S.C.A) was a regular conference of college and high school students who met to help advance the public face of the Faith. CISCA sponsored drives against the promotion of indecent literature and films and promoted positive programs for young people.

Social justice issues were not the sole property of the political left wing in American life, the plight of the American Indian was addressed in 1938 and active support through the Home Missions went directly to the American and Canadian Indian Reservations – long before Marlon Brando trotted out an ersatz "Indian

Princess" at the Academy Awards. Joseph Henry Morris, Head Chief of the Iroquois Indians of the Six Nations addressed the students of Leo High School on December 6, 1938. Mr. Morris was the first American Indian chosen to the All American Team in 1905. He later appeared in movies like "Union Pacific" and "Hiawatha." Chief Clear Sky Morris condemned the portrayal of Native Americans as blood-thirsty savages and debunked the myth of the Indian massacre. Chief Clear Sky Morris concentrated on the deplorable conditions Native American Reservations.

As opposed to Marxist soap boxing, the delegates of Catholic action raised practical issues of social justice like crashing dances, shop-lifting, vandalism, and dogging it on the job. As most of their families had spent time on the picket lines, the right of workers to organize was inbred with the Catholic faith. Issues of economic justice began with us and not the rise of a revolutionary tide. Bishop Sheil and CYO directed food drives, mission collections, helping the homeless, elderly, and maintaining some standard of good behavior seemed to work for the greatest generation. While the rhetoric of the Red left during the Depression is valorized by the leftist romantics , the hard copy available in the pages of *The Oriole* reflects a social activism rampant in Catholic Chicago.

The simple truth of 'deeds not words' continues through the life of Leo High School. The students were challenged, but their Faith was never questioned. It was an *a priori* commitment to the faith of their mothers and fathers that allowed Leo men to challenge themselves in the classroom, on the athletic field, and in rare moments of quiet reflection. Thirty Nine (39) were ordained priests. Thirty two others became Irish Christian Brothers:

1960 Football

Brother Finch

VI.   The Lay Teachers – Cuts of Same Solid Cloth as Their Students

These Chicagoans were no milquetoast Catholics. 1943 City Championship Lion guard James C. Arneberg who would lead the Leo football in the mid – 1950's was a daily communicant. Arneberg joined the Marines after graduation (twenty three members of the Class of 1943 were WWII Marines) and served with another Chicagoan, Izzy Cagan a west-sider and a Jew. After both men were wounded during the fighting on Guam they were sent to a rest camp. They were visited by fellow Chicago marines from the south side (Dick Burke, Dick Prendergast '43, and a St. Rita guy with the 3rd Marines. Cagan told Pat Hickey (St. Rita '43) that he was required to attend Mass every morning with Jimmy 'just in case.' 'Jimmy, for Crissake, I'm a Jew!' Arneberg would dump Cagan's cot into the slit trench in their tent, if Izzy ignored Jimmy's call to services. At Arneberg's funeral Mass in 1985, Cagan also explained how this courageous and committed Lion saved his life in the fighting on Guam. Cagan had been hit by a flame thrower and Arneberg smothered the flames with his body and then carried Cagan to an aid station under heavy fire.

Arneberg as coach of Leo football stressed devotion and self-sacrifice. Jimmy was shot up and bayoneted in the fight for Okinawa, but recovered to claim football honors at Loras College after the war. Jimmy then joined the faculty of Leo High School as an English teacher and coach. His players would compete fiercely and were coached to be Christian gentlemen: No Girls! No Cigarettes, No Swearing! But sweat all you like. (When I was about five my Dad took me to Foster Park and there I watched Jimmy Arneberg launch himself onto his hands and run on his arms through the park gate on Bishop Street, through traffic, across 83rd Street to where our car was parked.) Jimmy Arneberg would kick players off the field for using 'bad words.' Talk about muscular Christianity!

The laymen like their colleagues the Christian Brothers instilled the values of the faith in their students. Profs. Allegretti, Davido, Topa, Doll, Reincke, Hession, Hanlon, Blide, Dowd, Joyce, Cummins, Fitzgerald, Tansey, Parker, Swazt, and . . . are remembered for their character and courage. They put their students before themselves. Their kids ate baloney sandwiches and vacationed at Rainbow Beach. Their kids got their clothes at Zayre's or Goldblatts instead of Marshall Field's, Lytton's, or Baskin's. Their wives went to Leo games instead of dinner at Don Roth's Blackhawk or Chez Paul's. Catholic school teachers made (make) appallingly low salaries and received very few if any fringe benefits. During the Depression years, lay teachers took $200 to $300 cuts in salary: from a princely $ 1,200 annual salary in 1931 to $ 900 & $ 1,000 in 1933. The average salary in 1966, had jumped to an astounding $ 3,000. In 1968, there was an attempt to form a Catholic teachers union. There was even a brief work stoppage. The union was 'broken' because the members themselves were committed to the mission of the Catholic schools. They wore ties instead of collars and had to endure the daily obstacles of ignorance and innocence. The lay teacher (called Professors in the more respectful 30's and 40's) was often an Alumnus and also a product of the same parishes as his students.

They shared the same identities as their students – Catholic Americans, working class Democrats, White Sox, / Chicago Cardinal /Notre Dame Fans, and committed to their jobs. They faced greater disciplinary challenges from their charges as a chewing out from a layman had far less cache than a dressing down from "The Brothers." Bob Hylard ('47) recalled that students were often more of a challenge to lay teachers than to brothers. "We would find the chink in the armor – nervous tick, a limp, a speech impediment, or some little thing in the poor guy's demeanor and give him hell." Command of subject matter is the key to discipline and Leo High School has been blessed to have teachers who were disciplinarians of best kind. A person who really loves to let others in on the secret of what makes him tick is a great teacher. Someone who sparks the intellect and fires the blood to exceed one's efforts is a teacher. Leo Henning commanded the instant attention of his students through his love of music and his command of its rules. In the same way Bro. John O'Keefe taught the practical applications of the principles of mathematics and algebra. It is said that he never needed a text book – but used one. Tom Joyce made *Beowulf* as poignant to a 14 year old as *Catcher in the Rye*. Brian Tansey ignited the spirit of 'good citizenship' beginning with behavior in the halls. Mr. R.D. Parker is remembered for his devotion to history and the Leo students. Along with Bob Hanlon and Jimmy Arneberg, Lou Narish helped Leo guys build their bodies and their self esteem in the gym. The great teachers never worked a day in their lives.

Mom and dad would give a real trimming to the young punk who gave lip to the Brothers or the teachers. Accountability is what formed character. The turn over rate among lay teachers tended to be high in the early years and therefore the longer a layman continued in his duties the more honor he was afforded. Teachers like Charles Reinke who taught business and coached bowling from 1929 until 1972 and Ray Blide who taught from 1930 until 1966 are universally respected by Leo men. Bob Hanlon served Leo from the time he ended his career as a professional football player in 1956, until his death in 1992. Today, all teachers are laypeople several valiant women have ventured in the Lion's lair and have given their all to education. Nancy Finn whose brothers attended Leo taught for several years in the 1980's. (List the ladies) However, Leo's is a testosterone rich saga.

The "muscular Catholicism" that dominated the culture of Catholic Chicago from the time of Leo's founding and into this century accounts for the attitudes that impact on the financial support enjoyed by this school. The year Leo opened, 1926, was marked by the Eucharistic Conference of Chicago which dominated the city as much as the World Exposition. The Church in Chicago was building according to the dictates of Cardinal Mundelein who agreed with Chicago architect Daniel Burnham to "make no small plans." Joseph W. McCarthy was assigned the design for Leo High School. He had become the unofficial architect for the Archdiocese when he was recruited to plan St. Mary of the Lake Seminary. A Leo graduate John J. Fox ('36) would follow McCarthy as the architect of most the schools and churches built by Catholic Chicago, from the 1950's through the 1970's. Catholics were competing in America. Notre Dame Football was the acme of sport. Roman Catholic Al Smith would run for President. Leo High School would dig its cleats in for a very long run.

Leo High School was originally a three story structure facing the streetcar lines north along 79th Street between Peoria and Sangamon Streets. At the core of the school was the chapel of St. Leo which served as an auxiliary to St. Leo the Great Parish. There was a swimming pool in the basement along Peoria Street connected to a cafeteria and power plant. Steam heat provided warmth to the original three floors of classrooms, labs, library, and gymnasium. At the corner of 79th & Sangamon were offices for the business and administration of the school. In 1926, it was a state-of-the-art school. The northern façade of the school were dominated by roman columns and large heavy doors. Enclosed by a wrought iron gate seventy years before Mayor Richard M. Daley's Chicago landscape dictates, Leo High School highlighted the vigorous life along 79th Street.

79th Street, according to the study of Catholic parish life by McMahon, had everything 'from obstetrician to mortician.' It is stated that people did 90% of their shopping along 79th Street: Tailors, dentists, candy stores, jewelers, sporting goods, meats and vegetables. The communities along 79th Street were worlds unto themselves, not unlike the Hispanic and Asian communities today. The centers of life were the Catholic parishes. McMahon records an anecdote about a student at Calumet High School in the 1960's. One young guy asked another where he lived and his friend replied "St. Ethelreda." The answering boy's father heard the exchange and asked his son why he answered that way and his son replied "How else will he know where I live?" The boy's father was the Lutheran pastor at the Church on 83rd & Paulina. There were so many Catholics at Calumet High School that it was known as "Our Lady of Calumet." Calumet also became the high school of choice for Leo students who fell from grace with the Brothers.

Streetcars and buses were the second most important means of transportation for Leo students and the walking the dominant. Tom Parson's '30 walked and ran three ½ miles to the street car stop on Western Ave. from his home in far south Blue Island to get his Leo education. There was very little to worry about in those days. Crime was unusual. As the neighborhoods were predominantly Catholic and ethnic (Swedish/German) Protestant there was general amity among neighbors. Many young men walked and even ran to school. Very few families owned cars until after WWII and public transportation was dependable. There were a number of tragic deaths due to traffic and streetcar accidents. POST from *Oriel*.

Frank Considine ('39) and Andy McKenna ('47) would take as many as four streetcar changes in order to get to Leo High School. Getting to school on time was only the beginning, once arrived a young man was expected or compelled to perform. The result was that Leo students found themselves on the bright path to future success. That path however was littered with challenges.

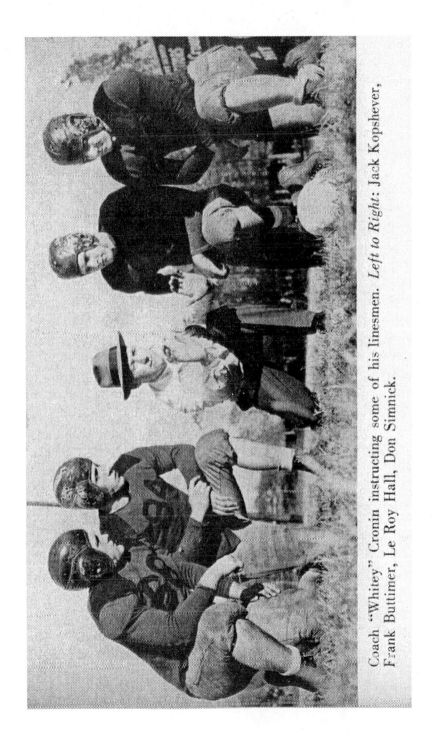

Coach "Whitey" Cronin instructing some of his linesmen. *Left to Right:* Jack Kopshever, Frank Buttimer, Le Roy Hall, Don Simnick.

B-25 Flown by Tom Gerrity

VII.   WAR II

Having survived the Great Depression, in no small way due to the efforts of Cardinal Mundelein and his brilliant vicar Bishop Sheil, Catholic Chicago started to get back on its feet. Pastor Shewbridge had wanted to kill the school's debt and also add on another floor to the existing plant, but the economy balked any such move. Bishop Sheil through Mayor Kelly had developed a strong association with the Roosevelt Administration. Cardinal Mundelein was a powerful supporter of the President's recovery programs and was the first American churchman to publicly vilify Adolph Hitler. Mundelein lampooned the monster as an 'Austrian paper-hanger and a bad one at that.' Cardinal Mundelein died in 1939 and was followed by Cardinal Stritch. Just when America seemed to be getting off the canvas, the Pacific Fleet was clobbered by a sneak attack.

Leo got its licks in: Ray Jelhi '39, who reported to St. Peter on February 2, 2004, was part of USS Yorktown's Bombing Squadron Nine. In the South China Sea, on April 7, 1945 Ray Jehli sank a Japanese cruiser. Leo High School sent hundreds of its men into the war.   Leo's War dead indicate the level of sacrifice willing to be put forth. Great athletes and scholars were now called upon put their talents and virtue to the supreme test.

Medal of Honor recipient John Fardy '40 smothered a grenade with his body in order to save his comrades, on Okinawa. Navy Cross Marine, Joe Auman '40 was killed manning a machine gun, while covering the withdrawal of his squad. Larry Spillan '41 was a member of the same Marine Raider Company as Auman and was killed the very same day. Martin Tully '30 won the Silver Star and was personally decorated by Gen. Mark Clark and later had a private audience with Pope Piux XII. Leo Airmen Army, Navy, & Marines account for the greatest number among the school's War Fallen. George Karl a Marne fighter pilot was killed when debris from a bomber had just shot down damaged his plane. George Karl was killed months before the end of the war and had managed to survive most of the fighting in the Pacific. The same guys who won the Catholic league and City Championships were now beating world fascism. Bernie Ingersoll the *Oriel* Sports Editor and columnist of *The Lion's Lair* was wounded in the fighting in Belgium and recuperated in England along side his former teacher Mr. Blide. Several *Oriel* notices of deaths in combat follow: *Attach*

From Dec. 1941 to the War's conclusion Leo Lions fought and bled in every theatre of combat. All through the War Leo dominated the sports pages and continued to send scholars on to the great universities as well as into military service. Their contributions to America were no less important than the sacrifices of the many in combat. These men would help to pave the path of peace – many as religious, Like Bishop John Gorman '43 and Brother Al Houlihan CFC '44. Having saved the World, the 'greatest generation' came home to more challenges and opportunities. The GI Bill of Rights gave working class guys an opportunity to get a college education. Marine Vet Dick Prendergast '43 returned to Chicago's DePaul University and become an attorney and CPA. The 'good jobs' on the street cars and in factories were now overlooked for careers in law, medicine, accounting, and business. With these new careers came greater opportunities to afford homes in Beverly or in the new phenomenon – the suburbs.

Bob Foster

Bob Kelly

VIII.   '50 through the 80's Happy Days and Historical Changes

During the War, the issue of affordable open housing in Chicago became thorny and of paramount concern. Available housing to African Americans remained limited to the Black Belt, until Mayor Kelly's administration. Mayor Kelly owed much to the loyalty of Blacks to his Democratic administration and ordered Chicago police to defend the rights of Black Chicagoans to own or rent wherever they so choose.   This created tensions in the white Catholic communities on the south side – St. Leo Parish in particular.   White middle class families elected to move to the newly created –rather fabricated – communities outside of the city.   Park Forest, Oak Lawn, and Evergreen Park now held an allure to former residents of Gresham (Spinney pp 204- 209). The Korean War took many WWII vets back into service and Leo graduates followed their older brothers into combat once again.

Through the 1950's, racial change became the dominant wave of life on the south side. The Catholic ghettos – like Auburn, Highland, Gresham – became more and more Black ghettos. In 1949, Monsignor Peter F. Shewbridge died. Four years after World War II, Leo's

63

founder had paid off the parish debt and planned the new home for the Christian Brothers. The courtly and pious Shewbridge was replaced by the flamboyant and notorious Monsignor Patrick J. Molloy. Pastor Molloy was no friend of fair housing and an avowed racist. He was also an astute politician and a guy who got things done. He ruled his parish like a Lord – he was 'the man' and he knew that every favor had a price to be exacted. Police and fire appointments happened or not because of Father/Monsignor Pat. He could raise money and "awareness." Father Pat did not park his car – he tossed keys to the nearest police man on duty whether it was at Comiskey Park or Holy Name Cathedral. Chances are that Sgt. Muckinfuch's job was made possible through a call downtown from Father Pat. There's juice and there's **juice.** Pastor Molloy immediately built the monastery at 79th & Sangamon and worked to preserve the racial integrity of his parish and he let the Christian Brothers know, in no uncertain terms to whom they owed thanks. God heard prayers and Father Malloy answered them.

By the early 1960's Chicago had a new Cardinal in Albert Meyer and the Roman Catholic Church a revolutionary Pope in John XXIII. The Second Vatican Council was convened to reexamine the faith and future of the Church. Arguably this was the most important and divisive move by the hierarchy since the Reformation. To the lay Catholic it seemed a very confusing and unsettling action.

The Mass in the vernacular, the role of the clergy, and the forms of worship which had been such a constant were now cast into the vortex of change. Moral issues like civil rights and birth control became dominant themes. Homilies by newly ordained priests seemed to be more sociology lessons than treatments of the gospel narratives. People were urged to question – any and all things. President Kennedy, the first American Catholic was elected, and America was sending rockets into space. Televisions broadcast in 'living color.' The family kitchen radio became obsolete. Japanese transistor radios now broadcast 'hillbilly music' and 'jungle tunes.' More kids sought deferrals from the military draft to go to college. Blacks and whites were moving closer together – in proximity if not harmony. A new 'undeclared war' in Asia took the place of Korea –Vietnam.

Like Korea, the forgotten war, Vietnam would claim the lives of Leo graduates but also burnish the reputation of Lions at war. Thomas Stack, Jack Farnan, Jim Farrell, Jim Furlong, Rich Doyle, and many others were grunts in the jungles who brought home multiple decorations for valor. George Muellner became a fighter pilot and Gen. Jim Callaghan made the only combat parachute drop in that war. Bill Newman '58 was a navy fighter pilot in Vietnam and would later command the Blue Angels. Larry Anders fought in 'the brown water Navy' on a river gunboat. The Vietnam War took its toll but Leo men stood up it. Every year Leo High School, the only high school in Chicago to do so, honors America's veterans with a ceremony on the Friday before Veterans Day.

In 1965,a wreathe was laid at the War Memorial containing the names of Leo's Fallen that was erected by Leo Alumni behind the efforts of Jim Durkin '40. Four-Star General Thomas P. Gerrity '30 and Silver Star winner Martin J. Tully '30 were present for the dedication.

That same year, one of the great heroes of the civil rights movement was Father Jack Egan. Father Egan had a love/hate relationship with Father Molloy. When Egan and community activist Saul Alinsky were putting together Organization of Southwest Communities one of first persons enlisted to help was Father Molloy. This was a man who refused to bow to Canon Law and buried his boyfriend friend the gangster Dion O'Bannion. Father Molloy was the real deal. His authority drew gallons of water and he was enough of a politician to get in on a sure thing: racial change would happen and there was a new Cardinal coming to town: Cardinal Cody and Project Renewal.

Under Cardinals Stritch and Meyer pastors had a free hand to minister their flocks. When John Cody became Bishop in the 1965, that pastoral autonomy ended. Through the 1950's Pastor Molloy vowed that Leo High School would never admit an African American. Likewise, he attempted to 'discourage' home sales to black families. It is incredibly sad that such a talented and energetic man would waste so much time and energy denying his fellow man basic rights. Nevertheless, times and neighborhoods changed and changed rapidly. Monsignor Molloy now was an active member of the Organization of Southwest Communities.

In the 1960's the first Black students attended Leo High School. Eventually, *Micks* from Sabina's, *Pollacks* from John 'A God, *Loogans* from Queen of the Universe and *Dagoes* from St. Mary of Mount Carmel added other ethnic pejoratives to locker room banter. More importantly respect for human beings grew. These color and blood issues dissolved into the spirit of the Lion. There would remain antagonisms and occasional hostilities, but generally Leo students got along. In 1967, the only Black member of Leo High School's football team was unanimously elected captain by his teammates – Frank Butler. That said the south side of Chicago in the next forty years was not a garden of racial harmony. All the while St. Leo, St. Sabina and Little Flower turned from white Catholic neighborhoods to African American communities. White Catholics seem to culturally identify themselves in terms of parish and African Americans by community. Today St. Sabina's official name is –The St. Sabina Faith Community.

The Irish Catholic State Street -79th Street- which had been the home of the St.Patrick's Day Parade, was now African American and minimally Catholic. Through the 1970's parishes like St. Thomas More, St. Bede, St. Dennis, and the parishes of Chicago Lawn provided Leo High School with white students to balance the racial make-up. The Christian Brothers found it difficult to find members to staff the school. Fewer Brothers were willing to live in the monastery in the Black ghetto, when they could find a home at Brother Rice or St. Lawrence High Schools. Tuition costs began to sore and Archdiocesan subsidies diminished. Cardinal Cody immediately 'retired' the old Irish parish barons and sold off parish property. Little Flower High School was sold to the Chicago Board of Education in 1973 and never lived to see its twentieth anniversary. Little Flower Parish folded up like a Mickey Rooney marriage. Shewbridge Field had been sold by Cardinal Cody in the mid-1960. Things were surely different.

By the end of the 1980's, Leo High School was land-locked in an African American neighborhood that had deteriorated. Gangs and drugs now characterized the once vital 79th Street. In 1999, *Tribune* Sports Editor Dan McGrath '68 and his classmates organized the Cecil McClure Scholarship Fund in memory of their classmate and gang shooting victim Cecil McClure. McGrath and Lenny Moisan were Leo Basketball stars and Cecil was one African American student with no basketball ability. Cecil and McGrath formed a great bond and McGrath remembers him as a peacemaker in a time of great racial hostility. Cecil was gunned down by Disciples gang members in 1967. In 1999, Eric Ersery '99 had been accepted at the University of Illinois. While walking home from work at Burlington Coat Factory, Eric was killed by gang gunfire. The Cecil McClure Scholarship was established in response to Eric's murder. Crime in the neighborhood reached its peak in 1995, when beat

621 of the 6th District was named the homicide capital of Chicago. Alderman Terry Peterson was appointed by Mayor Richard M. Daley to replace 17th Ward Alderman Streeter. Terry Peterson reached out to institutional anchors like Leo to continue its mission and help renew the community.

Businesses and services left the community, but Leo High School remained as an anchor and provided some sense of stability. White families were not as willing to send their sons to Leo due to the dangerous nature of the environment. Mount Carmel High School continued to see sons and grandsons return, because the campus was blessed by the proximity of the University of Chicago, the parklands and the infrastructure afforded by the Metro station. Mount Carmel though in the heart of Blackstone Ranger turf is perceived to be a safer neighborhood. DeLaSalle Institute enjoys the same understanding. Leo's physical situation allows for limited campus expansion and bus routes in this neighborhood are notoriously dangerous.

The real story of Leo glory begins in 1991, when Leo as given no more than an another year of survival by Catholic School Superintendent Elaine Schuster. With the departure of the Congregation of Christian Brothers from Leo High School, white Catholic student recruitment ended. The fact of the matter is that Catholic parents in West Lawn, Beverly/Morgan Park, and the suburbs refused to send their sons into a dangerous neighborhood, when a religious order sponsored school was available. In fact many "legacy" Leo families sent their sons to Mount Carmel six miles further to the east and DeLaSalle eight miles north of Carmel in order to maintain that Catholic identity.

CLASS 1F
Freshmen

Row 1: J. Speiser, B. Golden, D. Lawrence, D. Sullivan, M. McManus, R. Weber.
Row 2: H. Powers, R. Seshan, J. Olsen, R. Shannon, R. Banks, D. Petelle, R. Sheedy, W. Janssen, W. Siciliano, J. Hardiman.
Row 3: J. Rose, W. Peters, R. Bartlett, T. McCurrie, J. Mereney, C. Newport, J. Foley, J. O'Shea.
Row 4: E. Cavanaugh, R. Moots, D. Furlong, K. McGarry, W. Ford, R. Kull, K. McBride, M. Burke, J. Geraghty, P. Rehder, C. Riordan, M. Derrane.

Row 1: K. Roberts, B. Hartigan, F. Wills, T. Fey.
Row 2: F. Conti, K. Dent, T. Boyes, F. Roach, R. Stepanek, B. Olsen.
Row 3: T. McBride, J. Harris, J. McCabe, R. Malonszar, D. Sullivan, R. Parrillo, R. Ring, D. Thoel, M. Reidy.
Row 4: J. Talbot, R. Taylor, R. Lewandowski, D. Stumpf, T. Messick, J. Ryan, D. Lynch, E. Drinane, M. Mortimer, J. Reitmaier.
Row 5: J. McMahon, E. Steglich, R. McNicholas, E. Keller, R. Perry, G. Boyer, G. Joseph, J. Kraft, M. Mantlo, J. Faulen, R. Morrissey.

CLASS 1G
Freshmen

1952

69

Mrs. J. Sauris.
Dramatics

Mr. L. A. Doll.
Registrar

Mrs. V. Utz.
Assistant Registrar

Br. W. A. Hennessy,
Science

Br. J. G. Keogh
English

Br. J. B. Walsh,
Physics

Br. P. R. Kiely,
Mechanical Drawing

1954

IX. Leo *Resurgam*

When the Christian Brothers left Leo, many African American parents called to complain that the Catholic identity must be maintained. For a number of years after the School added "Catholic" to its name in order to ensure that identity. Leo remains a Catholic school though most of its students are not. It is the Catholic identity and the parish sensibilities imbued in Leo alumni that maintains the powerful support. Foster due to his reputation as a leader who got more out of his people than any one expected became the key to holding on to Leo's identity.

Bob Foster grew up with Leo yearbooks instead of Golden Books. His older brothers, Tom, Jack, and Don had followed their father on the Chicago Police Department. Bobby grew up at 77th & Lowe being drilled by his brothers in Leo mystique: " Jesus, Bobby – Ike Mahoney was the first Leo Football coach and not Red Gleason! Horsey O'Neill never went to Leo ! Jerry Toureville went to Colorado after Leo." He was also challenged by his big brothers to block or tackle guys years older and shirt sizes bigger than Bobby. This early schooling in Leology would pay off. Bob Foster respected the support Leo High School enjoyed. He also witnessed the folly of doing a patch-work job on traditions.

In 1988, The Archdiocese of Chicago developed a hybrid concept for preserving a Catholic presence in the inner city. Mendel High School was abandoned by the Augustinian Order as a financially unfeasible. Once the site of the old Pullman Tech, the Augustinians developed a powerful Catholic high school to serve the south east side. With a campus and facilities that were the envy of the Catholic League, Mendel produced an Alumni body the equal to all other Catholic schools. The turbulent Sixties and the realities of race relations in Chicago took its toll on Mendel. Like Leo and other racially changing Catholic schools, admissions slowed and financial needs escalated. As with the Christian Brothers after them, a school with a solid identity and sense of tradition was cast aside. It was determined that in order to maintain a Catholic presence in the neighborhood Unity (Formerly Mercy), St. Wilibrord, and Mendel High schools would be merged.

Rather than reaching out to Mendel graduates for the respect due them for past financial and moral support, an attempt to manufacture an identity was put into play. The once magnificent campus of Mendel High School became St. Martin DePorres. You can't take a blue ribbon champion Landrace hog and run it in the Kentucky Derby, nor should a school's culture be morphed for pure expedience. In its brief life, St. Martin's never developed any identity and sucked millions of dollars out of the Archdiocese.

Quigley South was closed – no longer exists. Weber closed as well. By the time this narrative gets bound Holy Cross will be closed. The Augustinians took over the Quigley plant and the school is now St. Rita. All of the traditions and culture evolved at 63rd & Claremont have been injected at 79th & Western. With wonderful grace and dignity, the Augustinians have also co-opted the Mendel culture to further fortify this vital school. That was an honorable and damn smart move and this Leo laborer tips his skimmer to the person, or persons who completed that stroke.

The Archdiocese for the very best of reasons wanted to present the possibility of an identity, but the identity was already there.   The African American boys and girls of St. Martin DePorres never had an identity – were they Unity, Mendel, or Willbrord students?   The Campus was Mendel –the identity was Mendel's. Leo faced with the same challenges had three choices – close entirely, move and change its mission or tough it out.

No capital improvements had been made at Leo – the original fixtures were in place, antique electrical wiring, seventy year old plumbing, a leaky roof, unpainted classrooms, cracked masonry, and a demoralized staff. Most disturbing was a deficit of more than $ 200,000. Prior to the official departure of the Congregation, Cardinal Bernardin informed Leo High School that there would be no further subsidy given to Leo High School.   Coupled with outstanding tuition debts, declining enrollment, and no forthcoming subsidy the Brothers quickly ended any future sponsorship or official association with Leo High School.   Principal Brother Pat McCormick made heroic efforts to revive Leo's status, but he lacked support from his superiors.   Despite the operation of the school by the Congregation of Christian Brothers through the 1980's and continued Archdiocesan subsidies, Leo High School was a financial sinkhole. All that would change.

Robert Foster put in his papers for the job of principal of Leo High School.   He was not the Archdiocese of Chicago's first choice, but members of the Alumni Association behind President Jack Howard informed the Chancery that Foster was the only one.   As a side note, in my time at Leo, no one man has stood up for Bob Foster and Leo High School more than Jack Howard; often these two men were in complete disagreement.

Jack has been a rock! Jack was a major force in helping keep Alumni support alive through his leadership of the Alumni Association and participation on the Leo Advisory Board. The key to Leo's continued life has been Alumni support.

Bitterness going back to the 'white flight' days ran too deep in some of the Alumni. Many others were of the opinion that a layman would be hard pressed to do what the Brothers failed to do. More believed that the financial burden was too big for even Bob Foster's broad shoulders. Dr. Elaine Schuster told Foster that she hoped Bob would have a school at the end of the year. That was not the first time that he had heard that message. In 1969, St. Rita Coach Pat Cronin warned Foster not to return to Leo as a football coach. "You'll be buried there, Bobby," said Cronin. An accounting firm immediately hired by Foster told him that he would never make it through the year. It was tough. But there were plenty of tough guys out there who wanted to continue the scrap.

Bob Foster bridged the racial and cultural gap between the active white Alumni and the African American students and families Leo serves. Instinctively Foster drew on the strengths of school culture and capitalized on the vitality of Lion's spirit. Leo men responded to a challenge but would never back a loser. Bob Foster was anything but that. As player and coach, Foster had evolved as a master of technique and skills. His teams always manifested an intense understanding of the game and a willingness to execute when called upon. Great players like John Winters '69, Pete Kamholz '71, Ed Ryan '71, Bill Letz '70 John "Moose" Gilmartin '70, Mike Marks '75, Mike Holmes '75 , and Dan O'Keefe '91 would go on to become football coaches themselves. In the classroom Foster's love of history and government ignited interests that would commonly be ignored by teens. As an administrator, Foster brought to bear any means to strengthen the image and operation of Leo High School. As a guidance counselor Foster took the gray side of the rules in order to help a student succeed. In all of his efforts the point of entry for any action must be the heart of the student.

Bob Foster like his Leo brethren is the type of man who buys the very best nails before he considers the purchase of a horse to shoe. Breakdowns will occur but plans will be in place to remedy them long before they happen. On his sidelines, someone is prepared to take a broken helmet and fix it from a spare parts box with every tool and part needed without destroying the game. Foster's assistants had roles to play so there were not too many players on the field, or players at the wrong position. Leo might lose under Bob Foster but not for lack of motivation, preparation, or execution. One of the best receivers in Catholic League history is Bob Sheehy '71. Bob is Chairman of Leo High School Advisory Board he gives of his valuable time because he knows that every decision and action taken is rooted in the success of school.

Foster was told that he was on his own by the Archdiocese. He found himself frequently at odds with the Archdiocese Finance Office. Debts owed to the Archdiocese were *not* overlooked. Only recently, the Chicago Archdiocese has been pro active in support of Leo High School. Leo is recognized as a self-standing institution and the Office of Catholic Schools actively encourages its operations. But in 1991, Foster could not look to Superior Street for assistance.

Nor could Foster expect any support from the Congregation of Christian Brothers. The Order that began its Midwest operations at Leo, which was the springboard for Brother Rice and St. Laurence High Schools, wanted nothing to do with the school on 79th

Street. The Congregation argued that there were not "enough brothers" to staff Leo and that *four brothers* would be required to constitute a house on Sangamon. The monastery built by the Parish of St. Leo was abandoned and left to the school to dispose of and a summer home in Michigan City, Indiana that was paid for by the Leo Parents Club was immediately sold; thus severing any connection with Leo High School. The proceeds of that sale were never given to Leo High School. Retired Brother Francis Finch and Brother John O'Keefe refused to leave Leo. They, like the school itself, were on their own. The fire of Edmund Rice was maintained by Brothers Finch and O'Keefe and Bob Foster would keep the glow going at Leo.

Sixty Four years of Irish Christian Brother tradition continues at Leo not by the Congregation of Christian Brothers but through the boys they taught – The Leo Alumni. Many Leo Alumni continue to believe that the Christian Brothers still operate the school. The Celtic cross still remains in the school logo. Brothers Finch and O'Keefe adamantly refused to leave Leo High School and remained on the faculty. The Irish Christian Brothers, now called the Congregation, left the building constructed for them in 1950.

Brother Finch was called to Christ in 2000 still teaching chemistry, algebra and computer science. Brother John "Steve" O'Keefe drives in with me everyday. Bro. handles attendance, tutors in algebra, coaches the hurdlers, and tells the truth. He is the last of the Mohicans –the last Irish Christian Brother. A Bronx tough guy, Brother Steve (the Irish Christian Brothers have a tradition of calling one another by their baptismal names) continues the mission of Blessed Edmund Rice. Along with President Foster, Brother O'Keefe maintains Leo's identity.

So now the Brothers were gone, no Archdiocesan subsidy, a leaky roof, bum plumbing, multi-Code electricity, typewriters instead of computers, and a killer deficit were some of Bob Foster's problems. These were 'small potatoes' compared to Foster's number one concern- the safety and welfare of his kids.

The Gangster culture spawned from poverty and despair provided cash and identity. Like the beer-war hoods of 1920's, street punks took advantage of their own people through intimidation and violence. But the new gangsters were more heavily armed and readily inclined to murder any one. The violence was no longer interracial but self-directed. Black on Black crime soared during the 1980's. The now blighted 79th Street became a shooting gallery and Leo High School itself was in the line of fire. Drug traffic and turf control became the dominant concern for Leo High School. The Mom & Pop store on the northwest corner of 79th & Sangamon somehow got a hold of a liquor license and that spot became a point of focus for turf control. Police Beat 621 which includes Leo High School had the top homicide rate in Chicago, in 1995. Leo students were assaulted by gang members and too many (seven) have been killed in gang cross fire, since 1990.

Foster pushed gang members and gang 'wanna be's' out of the school and immediately introduced safety measures such as cameras, security doors, safety windows, as well as faculty presence on key corners during arrival and departure times for students. Teacher accountability for attendance was tightened. Visitors to Leo High School were admitted only at the security door on 79th & Sangamon. (One unwelcome visitor, a prominent gang-banger thug and so-called community activist, tried to bluster his way into Leo and was sent out the door by Bob Foster.) For safety outside of the school, Sixth Police District officers provided before and after school presence and beat cops made routine patrols of alleyways. Today, Officer George Newell '75 patrols the beat around Leo, attends every home game, dance, or gathering. George has thrown the bracelets on more than a few gang-bangers.

Leo High School, in the early and mid-'90s, was certainly not the Leo remembered by the Alumni but it was their school and these were *their* kids too. Dick Landis '47, Jack Howard'61, Jim Collins'61, Don Flynn'57, Andy McKenna'47, and Frank Considine '39 played a very active role in the initial moves to help the school get back on its feet financially. In the 1970's, Dr. Tom Driscoll'44, Bob Ward'61, Dick Prendergast'43, Matt Lamb'50, and the great Thomas A. Murphy'32 CEO of GM broke their backs to shore up Leo finances and put together The Leo Foundation. Benefit performances by Tony Bennett, Pearl Bailey, and other top flight entertainers helped the school meet expenses and too often payrolls. Doc Driscoll '44 is one of the most renowned pediatricians in the Midwest and founder of Palos Community Hospital. Through the 1960's , 70's, and 80's Dr. Driscoll served as Leo's team physician and was a major fund raiser through the Cadillac Raffle which averaged $ 25,000 in revenue to the school annually. Dr. Thomas P. Driscoll '44 continued his presence at football and basketball games and was on the spot anytime his advice was needed, until his death in Spring 2004.

Timothy McCarthy '67 saved the life of President Reagan when John Hinckley attempted to assassinate the President in 1982. Tim gets calls from Mrs. Reagan periodically in thanks for taking the bullets that would have been fatal to her husband. When President Reagan was leaving Bethesda Naval Hospital, with his characteristic kindness, he dropped by to visit the still recovering McCarthy. President Reagan counted on his fingers and said, " 1. McCarthy, 2. Reagan, 3. Brady, and 4. Delahanty (D.C. Police officer): what the hell did this guy have against the Irish? McCarthy continues to in law enforcement as Chief of Orland Park Police and is sought out by civic and fraternal organizations as a speaker. More often than not, Tim's fees find their way to Leo High School.

Bob Foster understood that support and goodwill were never born of sob-stories or excuses: Accentuate the Positive, Eliminate the Negative, and count out Mr. In-Between. Foster's gospel and fund raising dictum was tell the truth and try not to call in a chip. There was a small cadre of Leo supporters. Race was not a condition of support. These guys were Foster foundation blocks. The Alumni Association through Jack Howard boosted the Decal Drive and sent the proceeds of Alumni Banquet for Leo's use. Foster used the money offered by Alumni and the Association applied every dollar to its allotted need. Tuition was collected in a timely manner and all budgets were carefully scrutinized. Foster immediately hired Roche, Scholz, Walsh, and Scholz Accountants to do a monthly audit of all Leo finances. In 1991, Foster hired Automated Data Processing (ADP) to handle payroll (the Archdiocese did so too in 2003) and teachers and coaches needed to justify *any* purchase. 'How will this expenditure benefit the students?'

Foster sent out two letters, Campaign Leo in the fall and 21st Century in the spring, to all of the Alumni which numbered roughly eight thousand accurate addresses. In any of his letters, Bob never asked for a dime. He thanked the great guys for their love of Leo and accurately reported on what was happening at the school. Schools in the Archdiocese were closing at an alarming rate. Most notably Weber High School closed immediately after conducting a major capital campaign. Foster vowed that nothing similar would happen at Leo High School. Dick Landis '47, CEO of Landis Plastics, Inc. had been active in his support of Leo High School made significant contributions to the school's unrestricted operating capital and provided leadership in helping restore Leo High School finances. Jerry Toureville '47 a star athlete and officer of the Chicago Parks District asked how he could help. John Grant '42 a retired Beatrice Foods executive jumped aboard to help bring in foundation support. Leo guys popped up to help from all over the country – Jeremiah Sullivan President of Mayes department stores and Joe Byerwalter past CEO of United Airlines reached home from San Francisco. John Caponera '72 made stops on the Comic circuit – and his memorable Chicago Guy stint on McDonald's commercials – to drop a donation. Mike McErlean '74 sent checks from London. Notre Dame Legend Bob Kelly '43 made the drop from the mint fields of Indiana.

Catholic educators always seemed to look for magic genii – 'if only we could hit the Lotto.' A millionaire would pop up and save the day. One big hit was all we need. The guys who made millions of dollars did so slowly, methodically, and ethically – if they wanted to keep those millions. A new creature emerged in Catholic education, in parallel to the financial decline of Catholic schools – the Director of Development. At best, these creatures helped articulate the mission of the school and the vision of its CEO. At worst, they were institutional gypsies and non-profit network leeches. Nevertheless, with some reluctance, Bob Foster hired a director of development. When the interview was completed he informed the candidate, "If you hurt this school, in any way, firing will be the least of your worries." Foster's admonition should be a condition of employment in all institutions: Without pestering the Alumni Go Get Money! Foster compensated his staff better than he did himself and sought to retain the best people. Leo lay teachers continue in the traditions of Reinke, Blide, Standring, Joyce, Hanlon, Hession,

Davido, Topa, O'Keefe, Allegretti, Tansey, Mutter, Lenz, Fitzgerald, O'Malley, and Swast.

African American Alumni were sought out to mentor and teach Leo students and provide more of an African American proprietary sense of mission for the school. As in all things what is important are the needs of the students. One of the first additions placed in the school was an African American Heritage Room. With a grant from the Helen V. Brach Foundation, Bob and Carol Foster spent their summer vacation of 1997 painting, wall-papering and decorating 1,160 sq ft of Leo with African themed colors and contours. Foster balanced the budget and initiated an endowment fund as well. Bob and Carol Foster planted and watered the many impatiens in the courtyard around the Veteran's Memorial and the statue of Our Lady as well. Carol Foster, a life-long teacher in Catholic schools spent nearly as much time around Leo as her husband. Carol taught many Leo students in grammar school at St. Basil's and helped make the school homelike. Bob lost Carol to cancer in 2001; we share too much in many ways- we both married up. The warmth noticeable when entering this school is due largely to Carol Foster's decorating ideas.

Leo tough guys like Jim Collins and Jack Howard went twenty-four seven for Foster. Bob Sheehy, Rich Finn, Bill Holland, John Linehan, Jack O'Keefe, Jack Fitzgerald, Bill Payne, John Lucy, Jack Farnan, and Bob Ward put together an advisory board. Dr. John Lucy signed on to contribute his wealth of educational expertise as a long-time public school superintendent. Ben DeBerry, founder of Dock's Great Fish, who would direct Leo's efforts to inspire greater participation of Black Alumni, along with Corky Reams, Curtis Cooper, and Mike Holmes made phone calls and personal solicitations. Jim Collins guided Foster to Marquette University Development veteran

Pat O'Connell who helped identify top sponsors. Ben DeBerry spent the husky side of a year trying to spark greater financial support among African American Alumni. Ben is always ready to help Leo High School in any way. Dr. William Payne a technical engineer and department manger for Motorola Corporation is never too busy to make time for his Alma Mater.

At the more strategic level Frank Considine provided Principal Foster with corporate insights and practical approaches to effective management. More than any other Leo man, Frank Considine provided an MBA level of advice that far exceeded his many hundreds of thousands of dollars in gifts. Not far behind Frank Considine in terms of time, talent and treasure are Tom Owens and Andy McKenna. The late Tom Stokes declined a spot in the Leo Hall Fame despite providing hundreds of thousands of dollars in quiet support. At the top of the development pyramid, Bill Koloseike (auto dealer Bill Kay) and Don Flynn gave the most significant and consistent financial support. These men have given much more than a million dollars in support to Leo High School between them.

Again, the dollars go to scholarships and the projects for which they are requested. Leo High School is debt free. There has been no subsidy from the Archdiocese, though there is now much better support. A campus expansion of a new recreational field between Sangamon and Morgan has occurred for the first time since 1950, thanks to grants from Chicago Community Trust, Helen V. Brach Foundation and support from Alumni. Tom Zbierski a Gordon Tech grad mentored by Leo Man Tom Winecki'58, is a frequent guest at Leo High School. Tom coordinates Big Shoulders Fund activities for its President Jim O'Connor. O'Connor, though a St. Ignatius grad, is a 79th Street guy. Tom helps Leo identify scholarship needs. Leo operates the only computer based Algebra lab (sponsored by Frank & Nancy Considine) developed by the National Science Center Foundation in Illinois. Our students receive more financial assistance through the Big Shoulders Fund and Leo Alumni than most Catholic high students. There are nearly as many computers as there are students in the school and the Beaumont Foundation granted a Leo a thirty station wireless laptop computer lab, which will enable greater access to the internet for Leo students.

President Robert W. Foster does not attend conferences in New Orleans, Vegas or Reno and he is not a member of the City of Chicago or Union League Clubs. It is a challenge to get President Foster out of the school. Where another school CEO might find a round of golf with potential benefactors, dinner at Gene & Georgetti's with television news programmers, or making an appearance at the Fash Bash with Chicago's *glitterati* as essential to leadership management, Bob Foster sticks to the quotidian tasks of leading a school by example. The only person to arrive at Leo High School before Bob Foster is Vice Principal Larry Kennelly. No amount of self-serving lick-spittle in my blood (which is formidable none-the-less) can undo that truth. No man or beast is present in this school before Leo's Vice Principal. But Foster is right behind Larry Kennelly. Foster is not a member of any country club and does not hob-knob. That is probably why Tom Owens, Don Flynn Frank Considine, Andy McKenna, Joe Powers, Dick Devine, Mike Sheahan, Jim O'Connor, Jim 'Skinny" Sheahan, John Buck and other civic notables take his phone calls. Paul Vallas, former Chicago Public School CEO and almost Governor of Illinois, came to Leo early in his tenure as public school chief. He and Foster immediately hit it off. Vallas graciously touted Leo High School's operation under Bob Foster on Dan Rather's *Eye on America* focus on Paul Vallas. Now superintendent of Philadelphia public schools, Paul Vallas is a member of

Leo High School's Strategic Planning Board. There are other friends of Leo High School thanks to Bob Foster. Good example is John Buck.

John Buck is a Roman Catholic Texan, Notre Dame graduate and multi-millionaire real estate developer. Mr. Buck brought Nordstrom's to Chicago and was one of the principle forces in the North Michigan Ave. renewal. When Boeing came to Chicago they rented from John Buck Company. In 1997, John Buck came out to 79th & Sangamon to look over Leo's campus expansion potential. Mr. Buck put together a development team including Herve LaVoie of Denver, CO. as architect, Power Construction, and John Buck Company operations chief Bill Moody (Moody's daughter was a stand-out distance runner at St. Charles High School) to design and plan construction of a multi-purpose gym/academic center on the southwest block between Sangamon & Morgan – three buildings stood there at the time.   John Buck did this *pro bono*.

On the way down to Buck's office at Sears Tower, President Foster voiced concerns about lack of visibility and the renewed activity by the gangs on that corner. I listened and drove the Dan Ryan. At Buck's office his staff laid out six months of Construction & Engineering work, costs projections, and capital allocation plans. We are talking about hundreds of thousands of dollars in man hours and sweat equity. At the conclusion of Buck's presentation, Bob Foster issued his concerns about the safety of the Leo students and suggested that it might be better to just "move the plan across the street." That way the administration would have a better field of vision on the new facility. John Buck's left eye twitched a couple of times but otherwise remained calm. His Pan-Handle roots became evident to me anyway – were we, now, sidewinders?. I was thinking here was one guy you did not want to dry-gulch. He carefully repeated Bob's concerns for clarification and agreed to do another design – *one last time*.

I was on the verge of filling my Union suit. We got into the elevator and Bob said. "that was real good. That John Buck is one hell of a guy!" I practically screamed " Are you kidding? He's pissed!" " About what? It's for the safety of the kids. He knows that. Buck's got great talent there and they should have no problem punching in a few numbers. Calm down, you're like an old maiden aunt for Crissakes! . . . Do you think he's mad? Really?" I whimpered all the way home. Buck made one hell of a design –two to be exact – one that would fit north or south of 79th Street.

Due to the realities of the political world, Leo still holds those designs and needed to opt for an out-door recreational field. Two months after that meeting, Foster and I attended a speech by John Buck at the Fifty of Friday Luncheon, which is co-chaired by Bill Figel '72. Just a week before, Leo High School was short changed in a real estate article in a Chicago business magazine. The article author's chin dropped to the tips of his Florsheims, when he watched the Sun Times Developer of the Year cut through a sea of well-wishers and ink-slingers to crouch down with his arm around Bob Foster's shoulders. The reporter, who was very tough to reach the week before gushed "You guys know John Buck?" The Texas Domer told the reporter " Bob Foster's one of my heroes," end of interview. The career educator and the civic leader talked for quite awhile. Buck appreciates people who do for others. CEO John Buck and Corporate Vice President John Q. O'Donnell '68 continue to make personal and charitable contributions to Leo High School and have established the John Buck Company Foundation Scholarship. John Buck is a genuine Chicago guy – you don't see him breaking his neck to get his picture in Mary Cameron Frye's column.

That seems to be some people's priority. There are people who read about the work being done at Leo High School who jump in to help.

A little lady named Mary Pherigo called my office about an article that appeared in the *Sun Times* about Leo – I am pretty sure that its was Mary Mitchell's *Sun Times* article – and wanted to know more about Leo. I jumped in my car and headed up to meet this eighty plus woman, in the neighborhood way up on Belmont & Newland. Ms. Pherigo had never married and her sister had recently passed away. She had been born in southern Illinois and she and her sister worked in the offices of a steel plant. Mary had no other family, but she was taken by the story of Leo's Alumni support. Her two story Georgian was only a mile from Holy Cross High School. I sent Mary some articles and letters and called her every so often. She sends thousands of dollars to Leo and calls Bob Foster about the young men she helps.

Chicago Fireman John Meuris and Chicago Police Officer Jim King went to Arizona two years ago, to watch the Cubs spring training. They were Brother Rice graduates which would somewhat explain their interest in the Cubs. After watching the *Great Whines of Illinois*, they repaired to a purveyor of liquid refreshments. The fireman was with Engine /Ladder Company #129 at 81st & Ashland and the policeman was at the fighting 9th District. In the bar, a couple overheard their conversation. Mr. Michael Trauscht had grown up in St. Kilian's Parish and attended St. Ignatius High School and was now a very successful attorney in Tempe, AZ. The two young civil servants had been so flattering in their descriptions of the Leo students, that Mr. Trauscht called Leo the following day. Mr. Trauscht had followed the Leo band down Morgan to the football games at Shewbridge Field. The fact that Meuris and King were so young and spoke so well of Leo High School moved him deeply. He also sent a check for two thousand dollars to help a family in need of assistance and asked to be put on Leo's regular mailings.

Shortly after Bob Foster took over as principal, an elderly couple showed up one day in the summer. Don and Teresa Rohan had lived in this neighborhood and Don had retired from Trane Corporation. At the end of Foster's tour, the Rohan's gave the principle an envelop with 'a little something in it.' After a few days, Foster discovered the Rohans had written the first of many $ 40,000 checks. Mary Pherigo and the Rohans make things possible for people who will never meet them. They are not worried about that.

Ray Simon, President of the Helen V. Brach Foundation and Donald & Byrd Kelly were among the first to actively support Leo's mission. The great Terry Dillon of the Fred B. Snite Foundation is always up for Leo stories. John Donahue of the Arthur J. Schmitt Foundation has been a frequent visitor, as has Peggy Blandford, whose father attended Leo. Peggy directs W.P. & H.B. White Foundation. Mel Cooney calls regularly on behalf of the Cashel Foundation. Terry Dillon helps keep Snite Foundation support alive. Terry Enright's Clare Foundation makes a great impact. Bo Kemper of the Chester Foundation supports scholarships makes an impact on our students. The Andrew Foundation of Orland Park recognizes the importance of Leo work. The efficiency and honesty of the management of Leo High School have brought many new friends into play.

Leo is waiting for an African American foundation, or corporation to signal a new level in support. Leo Parent and African American construction contractor Lloyd Fuller alone contributes more than all African American Alumni combined. Not only that Mr. Fuller drives the bus to away games and is always there for the school. Every one asks, "What do you get from Oprah?" Indeed! So far not even a letter saying no. The same goes for the MJ Foundation established by the Bulls great Michael Jordan. Black real estate moguls, bankers, manufacturers, publishers, and civic leaders have all been asked to give support to Leo High School, but no assistance has been tendered. We have asked. We are still waiting. Two of Chicago's most influential African American real estate moguls, Elzie Higginbotham and Dempsey Travis praised the accomplishments of Leo students but declined to support them. Mr. Higginbotham spoke to the Durkin Leo scholars about his own struggles to succeed in December 2003, but did not offer to support scholars. Mr. Higginbotham is a member of DeLaSalle Institute's board of directors, of which Mayor Daley is a graduate, and may be too stretched to also support Leo; however, Mr. Dempsey Travis has no interest in supporting Leo. He told me that our next conversation will take place in that 'cabin in the sky.' All of Leo's foundation support and corporate support is white and with the exception of Andrew Foundation and Rueben Vernoff of Berner Charitable Trust, Roman Catholic. Chicago Community Trust provided the seed money for the first campus expansion in 50 years. Leo has yet to receive support from African American civic and philanthropic leaders.

Ada S. McKinley Foundation requested that Leo assist five students. Leo High School subsidized the total cost their tuitions. Four of the young men graduated from Leo High School in 2004. Leo High School should be celebrated and supported by Black Chicago but continues to be taken for granted. Leo High School serves the African American community and should be supported by it. *The Chicago Sun Times* Mary Mitchell wrote of the lack of support from the Black community back in 1996 but there has been no change in attitude. Since that time Leo has lost many great benefactors, like Mark Cronin

'42 a roofing contractor who organized the Class of 1942 Scholarship; Tom Stokes '54 provided $ 40,000 annually in tuition assistance, Frank Monahan '49 established a scholarship, as did Dr. John Phillips, Kevin Leo, Rich Nugent, The Class of 1951, Doc Driscoll, Dan Brennan and all of the others who made Leo their memorial beneficiary. The many flags to the right of an entry in the obituary columns should serve as a barometer. Bill Brennock '52 of Sherwood Oregon has contacted many Northwest Coast Leo men to contribute to the Spirit of the Lion Scholarship Fund. Dr. Hartney's Spirit of Lion editorial in the Oriel is maintained sixty years later. As the greatest generation comes into Christ's Kingdom, Leo's benefactors fade as well.

Leo High School takes *nothing* for granted. The school enjoys financial support unmatched in the school's history. The donations are managed and accounted for with painstaking accuracy. Most importantly, the fruits of the labor and the reason this school exists, the Leo students continue to make great records of achievement. President Bob Foster does not call in chips nor does he push tickets. Like his patrons, he believes himself to be a cog in the wheel of history. Foster's study of history and love of sport fashion his outlook. Lucius Cornelius Sulla, during the Roman Republic, explained why Romans had no king to representatives of the Parthian and Armenian Sovereigns: A man's greatness is measured only in proportion to the debt he owes to others. A truly great man does great things for others. A king is only concerned with himself, therefore a Roman is greater than a king. A man's actions (virtue) in life added to his dignity (*dignitas*) which he would leave behind and thus ennoble his family (*gens)* even greater. Romans outlawed kings, because kings could never get past themselves. This Roman Catholic school tradition welds Christ's gospel to Roman ethic. We are all small in Christ's plan but great in His operations. As such, in my ten years at Leo High School, I have never met a big shot, but I have met many great men and women.

As I mentioned before, Bob Foster is not someone who will ride a great horse unshod. The operation of the school like the management of any organization requires planning, preparation, and practice. Approximating the Roman legions, Foster's followers fought battles before they took place. Roofs will leak, paint will chip, pipes will burst, and equipment breakdown. The key lies in preparing for the future; Preparing to Succeed. To Bob Foster some of the most important individuals to Leo's success on the field and off were the guys who managed the teams. They were the before and after men who made things happen. They were not the big stars but the guys who made things happen. They became successful in their chosen careers, happy in their lives, and willing to be of service to others. They had the courage to commit. "For with every heart and hand, we will fight as one strong band/ For the Honor of the Orange and the Black."

> On Monday, March 15th Leo High School was in its second day of glory following its 1st Class A Basketball Championship and it was the day following the South Side St. Patrick's Day Parade. All of the news features about Leo's Triumph had been swallowed in the Sunday Editions, like so many pints at Keegan's Pub on Western Ave. From Monday on, Leo needed to look forward, as a team, as a school, and as learners.

It had been a sobering experience, in tallying the costs of going down to State. Rooms, transportation, and meals for players and coaches alone, totaled to more than $ 8,786. Coach Cannon, his assistants, and our players enjoyed the hospitality of the Pere Marquette Inn, Peoria. The Leo Men dined at pizza buffets, and ham 'n eggers. Average meal costs for fifteen players and their coaches amounted to $164   (@ $6.56 pp. Tax included – Tips came out of the Coaches pockets) . The kids obviously were well nourished given their performance on the hardwood.

As in any great celebration, there is the reckoning. Like the many Leo Men who enjoyed Bernard Callaghan's pintsmanship at Keegan's Pub on Western, (Judge Jim Perner '50, Jimmy Collins '53, Frank Monahan '53, Jimmy McDonnell '51, Ray Thompson '52, Dan Brady '62, Mark '86 & James McKenna '89 + Terry Earner '78 who delivered the product) March 14th, observed by Homicide Dick Billy Higgins, there is payment for the enjoyment. Now, Leo High School must dig deep for the very wonderful time that we all enjoyed in watching our young Lions dominate the basketball floor in Peoria. As director of development for Lec High School I thought you folks would like to know what it cost to compete in State Competition.   As Bernard Callaghan would say ' Time, Gentlemen!' Leo men stepped up to help: Lloyd Fuller one of Chicago's top African American contractors, wrote a check to cover most of the costs of transportation. Mr. Fuller has stepped up. One long-time Leo supporter Dr. Thomas Driscoll passed away just before post-season play began. Doc Driscoll wrote many checks similar to Lloyd Fuller's when Tom O'Malley and Jack Fitzgerald directed Leo basketball. It is sad that Doc could not have sat with Lloyd Fuller and the many Leo men who witnessed Leo's first IHSA Basketball Championship.   Bob Foster was tied up with school business that great weekend and had to settle for the television coverage.

Leo is more about doing the job than reaping the rewards. President Foster makes hundreds of calls and answers thousands of questions each week. Every payroll, time-sheet, purchase-order, requisition, invoice, and deposit crosses his desk before our accountants do the double-check. Bob Foster mirrors the people who built Leo and continue to support it – good people, who do not have an exalted opinion of themselves, but contribute to the building of a much better world. Foster knows that he is expendable and that is why he is so essential. Leo High School continues because people are challenged to have the courage to look beyond themselves, to look back on the accomplishments and sacrifices that are necessary to pave a path for those to come and the commitment to ensure that the work continues.

The Nature of the generosity that has been showered on Leo High School is rooted in the Catholic values and ethnic identities of its Alumni.

The nature of the Chicago Catholic parish, from the $ 50,000 raised by Irish immigrants in 1885 for the dedication of St. Leo III Parish to the $ 500,000 check written by Donald F. Flynn in 1994 for the restoration of Leo High School's physical plant, 'giving back' is the touchstone. This giving back is pure Celtic irony. Future generations are always the beneficiaries of this action: Give back to go forward.

The givers learned this art in the classroom, on the kneelers, and at the supper table:

- 'give your strictest attention to the lesson at hand,'
- 'give your heart and soul to Our Lord,' and
- 'give your poor brother a chance at the pork chops when he gets off work.'
- 'Give your ears a chance and learn something.'
- 'Give your best in the game. Put out! You get what you give! '

- ' Those to whom much is given, much is expected.'

In our toss- it - away society, the truth is brushed aside or dismissed as irrelevant or politically incorrect, or more than likely -inconvenient. Leo High School is supported 99.9% by white Alumni. Most Catholic schools enjoy alumni support as a tradition that is handed down generation to generation: St. Rita Men have St. Rita Grandsons, and Great Grandsons enrolled. Leo High School was an integrated school until the Congregation of Christian Brothers departed. With that the tangible connection to Catholic identity was severed. White Catholics continued the Catholic Connections at Mount Carmel, St. Rita, and DeLaSalle – all inner city schools with substantial African American presences. Leo High School remains a Roman Catholic school of the Archdiocese of Chicago. Its support comes from Catholics and it serves African American men.

This great high school will continue its mission only so long as it receives support. The realities are this: the biggest contributors to Leo High School are men from the classes of the 1940's,50's. & 60's. These men are aging and unless African American graduates and the African American community at large shore up the loss of income when these men pass away, support will vanish. Leo's Founder, Monsignor Peter F. Shewbridge, in his introduction of Cardinal Mundelein and Bishop Hoban at the Commencement of the Charter Class of 1930, stated

We have our school. It is a central high school . . . but the main burden in the undertaking depended upon the loyalty and the co-operation of those who will be benefited by it, and that I expect, and I know he (Card. Mundelein) expects. (Commencement Speeches , June 4, 1930)

Since 1991, more than five million dollars have been contributed by Leo graduates. Up to now those expectations have been wonderfully met. This was a story long over due in the telling.

Leo Athletics: Only a Tiny Sample

No challenge seemed more daunting than the opportunity to play football at Leo. Ike Mahoney, Whitey Cronin, and Red Gleason crafted the Leo football mystique as much as Rockne and Leahy had for Notre Dame. There were teams built around linemen like Ken Murphy, Dinny Reid, Joe Ziel, and "Skip" Carroll. These 'brawny stalwarts" gave the magical running back Johnny Galvins, Babe Baranowskis, and Bob Kellys the real estate necessary to perform great feats of athleticism before crowds of 10-20-and 100 thousand people. The largest crowd ever to attend an American football game witnessed Austin High School stun Leo High School in the 1937 Kelly Bowl. Johnny Galvin played the entire game with a broken arm.

Leo notched a reputation for football players who could take it, like it, and dish it out. Mendel great Terry O'Brien '59 stated that he "hated to play Leo, because guys like Don Flynn and Rich Boyle enjoyed doling out pain. Every game was life and death. Mendel had no cupcakes either but those guys at Leo were nuts!"

Leo Football was black and blue, though officially Orange and Black. Whitey Cronin who succeeded Ike Mahoney as coach was a lawyer who graduated from St. Rita High School. Like Mahoney, Cronin instilled a ferocity and love of collision in his players. Bob Kelly, Tony Kelly, Bob Hanlon, Jimmy Arneberg, and Babe Baranowski recalled the one time that Cronin ever dressed down the Leo squad. It was at half-time, during the Catholic League Championship game in 1941. Leo was beating Fenwick, but Cronin felt that he was witnessing a disgraceful performance. He lined up each player and personally read each man the riot act. They went out and won but they 'played much better football.'

1941/'42 Leo High School Football Season & Post-Season Play

Head Coach – A. I. "Whitey" Cronin In an interview conducted in 1995, Brother Finch who had served with every Leo football coach but Ike Mahoney declared that of them all Cronin was by far the very best. " He had an eye for talent moral I spiritual and athletic. To be truly great one needed the first two qualities more than the last.

Asst. Coach – E. Johnson

Catholic Central of Hammond V. Leo – 25-0

St. Patrick v. Leo – 27-0

DePaul v. Leo – 20-0

Mt. Carmel v. Leo - 34-7

St. Rita v. Leo 40-14

St. George v. Leo 21-0

St. Philips v. Leo 27-0

Joliet Catholic – 20-0

De La Salle – 19-0

Catholic League Championship Game – Leo High School's Third Consecutive Win

Fenwick V. Leo 20-0

City of Chicago Championship Kelly Bowl at Soldier Field Crowd over 100,000

Tilden Tech v. Leo 46-13

Season

11-0-0

Later coaches Joe Gleason, Jimmy Arneberg, Horsey O'Neil, Bob Hanlon, and Bob Foster would continue this fierce doctrine. Johnny Galvin '38 played the City Championship game with a broken arm. Angelo Prassa, Dan McGrath, Joe Gorman, Rich Budil, Ray Toploski, Morgan Murphy, and Horsey (who had a little brother Pony – you can't make this stuff up . . .) Cavanagh continued in this tradition through the 1950's. It has been argued that the 1954 football squad sent the most talent to the Big Ten, than any other Leo squad.

Don Flynn '57 played against Gordon Tech with a cast on his broken arm. A Gordon player begged the referee to do something about the guy trying to kill him. The Ref noticed a great amount of plaster mixed with blood on the Gordon man's face. Play continued nevertheless. Don Flynn went to Wisconsin on a football scholarship but tore up his knee, transferred to Marquette University, and went on to become one of the great entrepreneurs in America (Waste Management, Blockbuster Video, The Discovery Zone, Extended Stay America). Flynn's teammate Ed Ryan played against Fenwick the following week with his arm tapped to his torso. Coach Arneberg called for a pass play to Ryan. Leo won 27-13. Fullback Rich Boyle made every Leo opponent miserable all season - Ryan and Boyle were "Mr. Inside and Mr. Outside" The nameless monsters who received little or no ink from Chicago Sports Journalists Bill Gleason and Dave Condon are remembered by the guys from the Catholic League and the public school's best teams for making very long Saturdays and Sundays. When the lights went on Friday night games were just as violent.

Notre Dame had a great number of Leo men play for her. Red Gleason, Bob Hanlon, Bob Kelly, Tom Brennan, Joe Rosser, Tom Gallagher, Dan Payne, and Jay Standring. The Legendary Frank Leahy always looked for Leo men to muscle-up his Fighting Irish roster. Purdue lauded Johnny Galvin as its most outstanding freshman athlete, and would add Bob Foster '58, Bob Sheehy '71, and Corcy Rogers '91 to its list. The University of Illinois would feature Leo legend Henry "Babe" Baranowski '41, Bobby Standring '70, and Mike Holmes '75.. The Big Ten, The Ivy League, and the great independent universities honed in on Leo's talent beacon. Rich Finn '71 would go on to captain Brown University. Stafford Hood '70 is now Dean of the School of Psychology at Arizona State University. J. Dillon Hoey '59 would star for Yale and bond a life-long friendship with Vice-President Dick Cheney. In 2003, labor lawyer J. Dillon Hoey passed away but not before establishing a scholarship for the African American young men who wanted a Leo education. The first contribution to the J. Dillon Hoey Scholarship following Hoey's funeral came from Mendel opponent, Notre Dame '64 Captain, and Houston Oiler Eddie Burke. Burke had played against Hoey in the Catholic League and had formed a life-long friendship. Some of Leo's greats include Bill Koloseike, Ray Topps, Lou Narish, Jerry Toureville, Bill Nelligan, Ben DeBerry, Bucko McGinnis, Jim Corbett, Morgan Murphy, Stafford Hood, Rich Sims, Bobby Lake, Larry Sink, Bill Nelligan, Bill Letz, Frank Butler, Coe Francis,

Joe Campagna, Pete Kamholz, Tom Donnellan, Packy Fahey, John Winters, Paul Leahy, Dan Payne, All of the Marks Brothers, Irwin Hermanowski, Moose Gilmartin, Jimmy Shea, Kevin McEldowney, Jim Callaghan, and hundreds more. Larry O'Brien '77 was said to be 'one of the toughest, meanest and most dependable linemen in my time at Leo,' said Bob Foster. There continues to be courageous and committed Leo men. Their foes in the Catholic League also recognized the continuation of the Leo legend in 2003, when Dan O'Keefe's outnumbered Lions returned Leo High School to post season play.

Swimming: The Tank Leo's pool was a neighborhood feature that attracted many new students. The great athleticism required of swimming was too often overlooked by the sports pages. *The Oriole* did a pretty good job of making Leo men aware of the powerful contributions made by Leo swimmers and divers. Through the 1970's Leo swimmers added to Leo High School's standing as one of the most competitive schools in Chicago. Water Polo began to be an important interscholastic sport

In 1938, great swimmers like John McGowan, Phil Duffy, Newcomb Chambers, Bob Kelly, Joe Gerrity, Ed Busch, and Bob Lee dominated the regular season in Chicago's Catholic League and finished 3rd in the Championship meet under the eye of Brother Finch. The full complement of swimmers participated in both speed swimming and diving. Moose Mulchrone the Tony Lawless Award Water Polo coach of Brother Rice got wet in Leo's tank with guys like Bob Schemel, Brian O'Malley and Jimmy Ault.

Cross Country & Track: Jim McShane: Five State of Illinois Track Championships belongs to a school with no track facility. Ed Barry '32 ran against the great Ralph

Metcalfe who with Jesse Owens shoved the race myth in Hitler's face. Mike Pope and Terry McElligott lead the long distance men for Brother Willie Doyle's 1968 and '69 teams. The sprinters and hurdlers work in the corridors of the school and the shot put is practiced beneath the swimming pool. Leo runners have used the alleys and streets. When possible they move to a park. Leo High School is the only Catholic school to win the State Championship in Illinois's 110 year history of the event. For years Catholic schools were barred from participation in post season play in all sports. However, the IHSA saw fit to allow Catholic school participation in State Title competition, since the mid-1970. Catholic schools find themselves hamstrung by ever-changing rules of participation from IHSA. The great Ryan Shields '03 took away more gold than Morgan the Pirate in his four years at Leo. If Catholic school kids were not such tough competitors it seems doubtful that concerns of 'fairness' would not arise. Nevertheless, Leo won the Class a Title four times and the Class AA title once despite enrollment numbers voodoo rules.

Basketball: Leo's Bandbox Gym: Ike Mahoney to Noah Cannon: As competitive and physical as Leo Football Leo High School Basketball has the distinction of winning the National Basketball Title in 1945 under coach Brother Francis R. Finch. Coach Vince Dowd, Red Gleason, Jimmy Arneberg, Tom O'Malley, and Jack Fitzgerald are Leo legends.

But of all great Leo yarns, this is my favorite. In 1966, Tom O'Malley's Lions won the South Section Title which was covered on a local UHF TV Station. During the post game hoopla, the TV Sportscaster asked Capt. Jerry Shannon, 'What's next?' With the aplomb of an accomplished Chicago Catholic League Scholar/Athlete, Jerry Shannon replied 'Cold ones at Ryan's Woods!' Understated acknowledgement of the game well played. To the uninitiated, non-south sider, Mr. Shannon's cryptic announcement anticipated refreshment from chilled malted grain beverages at Cook County's Forest Preserve between 83rd & 87th Street along Western Ave.

In 1972, before Catholic schools were allowed to participate in the IHSA State Championships, Tommy O'Malley's Lions scared #1 ranked Hirsch into a closet. It was a great time to be associated with Catholic high schools. Jack Fitzgerald continued to put some of the best disciplined teams on the hardwood of Illinois – memorably his 1986 Team. Tony Rapold, Mike Manderino, and Jerry ToKars were a succession of Catholic League veteran coaches who directed the Lions after the departure of Jack Fitzgerald. Mike Manderino and Jerry Tokars both coached great Leo athletes like Andre Brown, Chris Burras, and Frank Clair. Leo graduate Noah Cannon who played for Fitz in the early 1990's took over as Leo's Basketball coach and won the 2004 Class A State Basketball Championship. Noah took no credit for the triumph but echoed the traditions of excellence and thanked our Alumni and the men who paved the path. Coach Cannon continued in the mold of Jimmy Arneberg in 2004/'05 by benching and later launching a blue chip player for showing disrespect to a teacher.

Ed Adams a Catholic War horse with more honors cluttering his apartment than anyone I know credits the kids for winning the track meets one event at a time and Brother Steve O'Keefe who keeps the boys focused on their jobs. Together Adams and O'Keefe have amassed five State Championship Track titles and too many Catholic League Championships to mention. As in every aspect of Leo life, committed and courageous people give every heart and hand.

I drive home - south on Vincennes to 107th Street- every night happy in the knowledge that at this one school people display their best qualities.   There are more prestigious and name-ready schools, but I know of no other place than 79th and Sangamon where the values that built Catholic Chicago are more in evidence. I have had more laughs and experienced more feelings of pride from my association with the great people supporting this school than any person should be allowed.   Jack Howard, Bob Sigel, Don Hogan, Art Skinner, Jim Collins, Mike Kelly, Mike Joyce, John Linehan , Bobby Sheehy, Rich Finn, Bill Holland, Dan Mc Grath, Jack Fitzgerald, Tom Durkin, Ben Deberry, Lloyd Fuller, Bill Payne, Al Townsend, Stafford Hood, Mike Holmes, and Mike Thompson – white and black men are orange and black men. The giants like Frank Considine, Don Flynn, Andy McKenna, Tom Stokes, Thomas A. Murphy, Tom Owens, Bill Koloseike, Doc Driscoll, Dick Landis, and Bob Podesta got their hands purified in the tough work of supporting this school as much as Jim Coogan, Rich Furlong, Larry Sink, Jerry Schmitt, Ken Lewald, Denny Conway, Jack O'Keefe, Billy Hickey, Tom Hopkins, Bob Cheval, Dan Stecich, George Badke, Ed Maloney Fran McCann, and Frank McDermott who attend every Leo event doing the deeds. Most of all there is Bob Foster whose rugged presence has preserved the values and traditions of Leo High School for almost fifty years. I have met many great men at Leo High School, but never a 'big shot.' This school is holy ground sanctified by deeds not words; everyone touched by those deeds is blessed.

Oriole Track Champs 1945

Top Row: Cronin (Coach), L. Prosek, J. Gallagher, K. Murphy, J. Frickenss, T. Woods, T. Brennan H. Bowen, R. Reiswicz, E. Stark, E. Johnson (Coach); Second Row: E. Soltis, H. Fleck, D. Lacoureux, J. Burke, B. Andruska, W. McElligott, J. Veeneman, R. Rowan, J. Casey, E. Lamb, W. Rowan, G. Brennan (Mgr.). Third Row: J. Hennesay (Mgr.), J. Dixon, W. Hinckley, Clarke, J. Fitzgerald, T. Byrne (Capt.), C. Hor, Heil, F. Ernst, J. Seahill, J. Callahan: Front Row: M. Mulcahy, A. Silius, L. Ryan, J. Farrell, W. Bohlman, J. Owens, J. Duig, R. Kiley R. Doherty, J. Donnellan.

1935 1st Cathloic League Champs

Capt. Frank Johnston headed for the goal in the game with St. Ignatius

MR. J. T. GLEESON
Football and Basketball Coach

1947

THE LINE

THE BACKFIELD

THE LINE: Left to Right
—Bob Bolmetch, Bill
Dunlap, Bill Ganey, Marty
Lawrence, Marty Flynn,
Jack Ziegler, Bob Mc-
Donald, Mr. Joe Gleason
(coach).

THE BACKFIELD: Left to
Right—Mr. Joe Gleason
(coach), Frank Johnston
(captain), Dan Henry,
Jerry Tourville.

1947

GRADUATES 1947
SENIOR HONORMEN

TOP: Geo Adlhoch, Jim Bergmann, Don Brown, Bob Crabb. MIDDLE: Joe Cunningham, Leo Flynn, Joe Geimer, Walt Kaiser. BOTTOM: Leo Kiley, Jim Mangan, Bernard McGinnis, Andy McKenna.

FACTA NON VERBA

SENIOR ACTIVITIES

GEORGE ADLHOCH, St. Sabina, Honor Roll 1, 2, 3, 4.
JAMES BERGMANN, St. Clotilde, Honor Roll 1, 2, 3, 4; Oriole Staff 4.
DON BROWN, St. Philip Neri, Honor Roll 1, 2, 3, 4; Oriole Staff 4.
ROBERT CRABB, Our Lady of Peace, Honor Roll 1, 2, 3, 4; Lion Staff 3, Oriole Staff 4, Swimming 1.

JOSEPH CUNNINGHAM, St. Kilian, Honor Roll 3, 4.
LEO FLYNN, St. Sabina, Honor Roll 1, 2, 3, 4; Band 1, 2, 3; Heavyweight Football 3, 4.

GRADUATES 1947
SENIOR HONORMEN

TOP: Dave McNamara, Tom McNamara, Joe McNitt. MIDDLE: Al Moran, John Murphy, Ed. O'Hara BOTTOM: Art Picard, Dave Powers, Ed. Proctor.

Richard Warman

LEFT TO RIGHT: Jim Stebbins, Bob Sullivan, Tony Verbiscar, Ed. Wysocki

BASKETBALL HEAVIES

Jim Minot   Ed White   Joe Gagliardi

Dan Halling (Captain)   Jerry Coyne (Captain)   Bill Kearney

Tom Wrenn   Dick Tulp

1952 Basketball Heavy

BASKETBALL LIGHTS

Ray Topolski (Captain)   Hank Beckman   Bill Kon

Harry Lee   Chuck Kelly   Pete Lynn (Captain)

George Dempsey   Dan Fetlow

1952 Basketball Lights

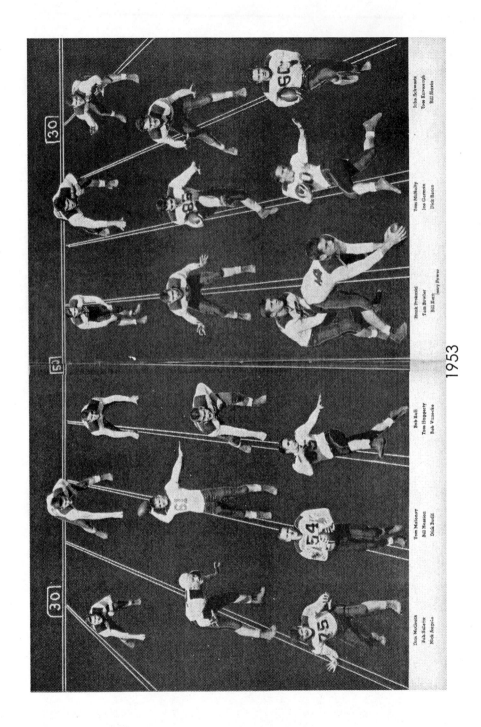

1953

John Schwartz
Tom Kavanaugh
Bill Simms

Tom McNulty
Joe Garmon
Dick Bacon

Henk Prakoski
Tom Bowler
Bill Kastt
Jerry Power

Bob Null
Tom Haggerty
Bob Viznocko

Tom Mahoney
Bill Hession
Dick Rudil

Don McGrein
Bob Sickerz
Nick Ampsio

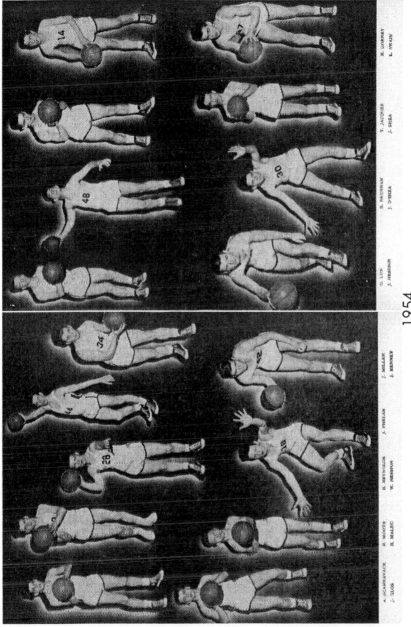

1954

LEO 20 MT. CARMEL 14

The Lions' wrath was felt in the special playoff game as the previous City Champions bowed their heads in defeat. The highlights were provided by Joe Gorman, Rich Budil, Jim Bushell, and John Schwartz all of whom scored for Leo. This victory ended a three year famine and gave promise of the Lions' return to its place at the top of the South Section.

SOUTH SECTION CHAMPS

1954

1954

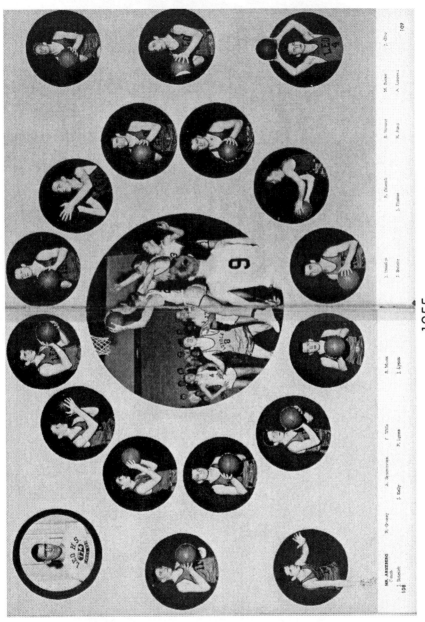

1955

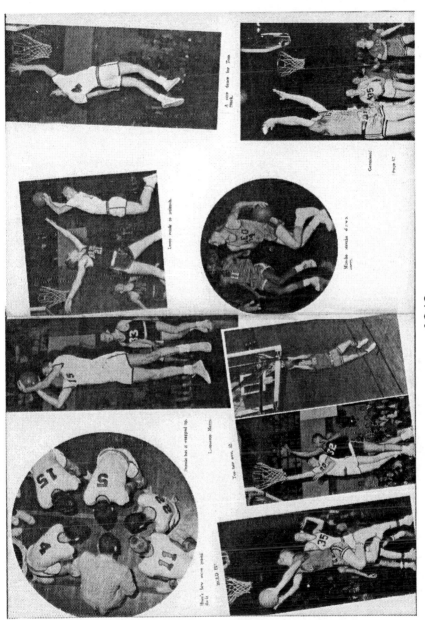

1960

115

Dr. Flaherty
Coach

TRACK . . .

The cindermen of Leo High School started off to another successful season in track by running in the school corridors. The senior relay team composed of, co-captain John Pendergast, co-captain Joe Clark, Gene Lash, Bob Hughes, and Ed Russell, was one of four teams that qualified out of ten different Catholic Schools for the Daily News Relays. A week later the Leo Relay Team took third place medals finishing third only to St. George and St. Ignatius, respectively.

Seniors returning from last year's squad who will lead the attack of the cindermen are: co-captain Joe Clark, co-captain John Pendergast, Gene Lash, Joe Bedali, Vince Wall, and Bernie O'Donnell.

Promising juniors who will also add depth to the team are: Ed Russell, Bib Hughes, Tom Dockus, David Cooke, Bob Peterson, Mike Wall, Harry Wilson, and John O'Leary.

While the senior team is leading their attack, the junior team will follow their example with the help of returning sophomores: Denny O'Connell, Ed Bauernfreund, Dick Smith, Kevin Westerkamp, Joe Mahoney, Tom Noel, and John Prinz.

Records Broken Last Year:

J. Mooney: outdoor mile	4:33.5	59	Senior
J. Mooney: Indoor mile	4:37.1	59	Senior
J. Clark: quarter mile	50.5	59	Senior
J. Pendergast: half mile	2:03.5	59	Senior
E. Russell: ¾ mile	3:26.5	59	Junior

Back Row: Raymond Blazyz, Albert Veith, James Farrell, Bernard O'Donnell, Gene Lash, John Pendergast, Jim Brown, Harry Wilson, Joey Badali, Richard Shag.
Front Row: Tom Dockus, Robert Hughes, Bob Peterson, Mike Wall, John O'Leary, James Smmanski, Jim Finan, Ed Russell, Vince Wall

1960

CHAPLAIN . . .

Father William Murphy, as chaplain of Leo High School, has been a source of help and inspiration to us all. He, and his able assistant Father Michael Hurley, have sacrificed much of their time to perform numerous acts to guide the students to a holier life; among these, hearing confessions every week and celebrating Hold Mass on First Fridays. For all this the entire student body and faculty extend sincere thanks.

Father Murphy
Chaplain

Sister Lucretia is shown with her "children" at Guardian Angel home.

1960

Freshmen—

(Continued from Page 1, Col. 4)

St. Rita 7

W. Le Mieux	L. Senica
D. Moss	J. Devine
E. Kelly	J. Daly
	T. Gibbons

St. Ethelreda 6

C. Fitzpatrick	J. Mooney
J. Dineen	B. Witry
R. Sheehy	E. Parker

St. Joachim 6

E. Gallagher	J. St. Ville
S. Flaherty	J. Brennan
J. Maroney	A. Altenbach

Sacred Heart 6

C. Horath	T. Rochford
F. Horath	R. Kennedy
M. Mahoney	R. Selvage

St. Margaret 6

W. Daker	J. O'Sullivan
R. Picard	J. Burns
E. Peters	D. O'Connor

Our Lady of Peace 6

J. Grace	W. Sullivan
W. Dillion	R. Cronin
J. Connors	T. Gibbons

Holy Rosary 6

C. Mulvenna	R. Murray
C. Esterhammer	H. Savard
	B. Brouillette

St. Bride 6

P. Gerrity	R. Coughlan
G. Rieg	R. White
D. Coughlan	R. Horka

St. Barnabas 6

J. Burke	W. Lee
B. Fanning	W. Hartigan
H. Richards	J. Rogers

St. Gabriel 6

E. Hillgamyer	T. McGrath
G. McElligott	M. McKeone
R. Danaher	J. Kelly

St. Philip Neri 5

R. Casey	L. Poglitsch
J. Carmody	R. Hanlon
	J. McAndrews

Parish Leaders

In the second Honor Roll of the school year 1939-40, St. Sabina and St. Leo led all the grammar schools represented in the Freshman Class at Leo. They are tied with eight each, who averaged 90 per cent or above in the quarter's work.

There were also dead heats for second and third places. St. Rita and St. Dorothy each boast of four honor students, while Little Flower and Our Lady of Peace have three to their credit.

St. Bernard's, St. Margaret's, St. Columbanus', St. Brendan's and St. Joachim's all are represented with two honor students. Fourteen other parishes have one each on the Honor Roll.

St. Leo (8)

Vincent Carroll	Edward Nelson
Michael Shine	Robert Madden
Thomas Curley	Donald Murphy
James McLellan	Edmund Connor

St. Sabina (8)

Roger Arzbaecker	Edmund Whalen
Raymond Schmit	Joseph Mullarkey
Robert Schmit	Robert Burke
Robert Miller	Roger Robinson

St. Rita (4)

William Lemieux	Leo Senica
Donald Moss	John Moran

St. Dorothy (4)

Michael Kielty	Edwin Sweeney
Thomas Conway	Albert Dahlke

Little Flower (3)

Robert Wall	John Sarsfield
	John McNicholas

Our Lady of Peace (3)

Robert Cronin	Thomas Gibbons
	John Connor

St. Bernard (2)

James Devane	John Morrissey

St. Margaret (2)

Jack O'Sullivan	Edward Peters

St. Columbanus (2)

Thomas Collins	Bernard Ingersoll

St. Basil 5

A. Battaglia   M. Boland
R. Carr   T. Whetherhult
     T. Gibbons

St. Columbanus 4

T. Collins   B. Ingersoll
R. Byrne   D. O'Connor

St. Bernard 3

.. Morrissey   R. Corlett
     J. Devane

St. Clotilde 3

D. Moynihan   W. Leonhardt
J. Hartman

St. Michael 2

J. Pierzchalski   F. Rozewski

St. Joseph 2

J. Bernal   R. Westort

Visitation 1

J. Gorman

St. Gall 1

P. Henry

St. Felicitas 2

W. Riordan   R. Mayer

St. Francis de Paula 2

J. Barlow   R. Philpott

St. Agnes 1

D. Nist

St. Adrian 1

G. McNicholas

St. Martin 1

K. Lucas

St. Bartholomew 1

R. Smith

St. Sebastian 1

F. Anderson

St. Mary Magdalene 1

G. Bocian

Christ The King 1

R. Murray

Holy Cross 1

E. Clare

St. Ailbe 1

P. Neylon

St. Nicholas 1

J. O'Rourke

St. Kevin 1

E. Rafferty

St. John Baptist 1

St. Brendan (2)

Robert Kelly   Robert Hanlon

St. Joachim (2)

Joseph St. Ville   Joseph Brennan

ONE HONOR STUDENT EACH

Visitation—Jack Gorman.
St. Gabriel—Joseph Kelly.
St. Barnabas—William Fanning.
St. Mary Magdalene—Gerald Bocian.
St. Gall—Patrick Henry.
St. Basil—Thomas Gibbons.
Holy Rosary—Charles Esterhammer.
St. Adrian—William Maguire.
Our Lady Academy (Manteno) — R. Knight.
St. Bride's—Robert Coughlan.
St. Joseph—Joseph Bernal.
St. Agnes (Chicago Heights) — D. Nist.
St. Carthage—Lawrence Hogan.
St. Felicitas—William Riordan.

C. Gordon

St. John 1

J. Etzkorn

Nativity 1

L. Patrick

Our Lady of Lourdes 1

J. Garry

All Saints 1

J. Gallagher

St. Theodore 1

R. Potesta

(Continued in Col. 4)

About the Book:

This is the greatest story never told. The guys who attended Leo High School are too busy doing to have time to do any telling. The story of the support for a school that everyone but Leo Men predicted would close or should be closed is a great Chicago story, a great Catholic story, a great human story, and a real American story. Not having graduated from Leo High School, I am free to make a big deal of what goes on at 79th & Sangamon on the south side of Chicago.

Leo High School is situated in an African American neighborhood, Auburn Gresham, but receives no active support from the black community beyond black graduates of this school. Generations of white Catholic men actively support a school that they attended, in order to help young black, mostly non-Catholic young men. None of their grandchildren or sons attends Leo, but they actively invest hundreds of thousands of dollars annually. These same supporters have been cast as 'white flight bigots' by academics, journalists, and even some religious. Mopes that hurl that charge go unanswered too often. Our people support Leo out of love for their fellow man – the same motivation that built the Catholic Church in Chicago. Without the support of Leo's Alumni, white and black, thousands of young men would not have the opportunity to succeed beyond the streets.

Since 1991, 93% of all Leo graduates have gone on to Purdue, University of Chicago, Boston College, West Point, Northwestern, Loyola, DePaul, Illinois, Wisconsin, Michigan, Michigan State to name a few. Others like Lonnie Newman '02, deferred college scholarships for the trades. Lonnie Newman, Class Valedictorian turned down six scholarships to join Pipe-fitters Local 597. No student is turned away from Leo High School – most students score below the 40th percentile on the entrance exam, but after four years of hard work and commitment go on to some of the best schools in America. Most of all, their tuition is supported by the Leo Alumni, because Lonnie Newman's story is familiar to them.

You won't hear about Leo on Oprah or read about it in Chicago Magazine. It is not a story for the slick or the showy. Leo people tend to sit in the back pews, even though they could stroll to the roped off section. They give away the fifty-yard line tickets and watch the game at home. They go to bat for a young man who needs a door opened for him. They live by deeds, not words: courage and commitment.

Dedication:

To the committed and courageous people of the greatest generations – the people who use their time, talents, and treasure to help those who will come after them; Brother Francis Finch CFC, Brother John Stephan O'Keefe CFC, Robert W. Foster '58 President of Leo High School, the generations of religious & lay staff, men and women, who gave so much to young men and all the Leo Men who live up to the mission of Blessed Edmund Rice.

Thank You:

I wish to thank the late Patrick J. Cleary, Publisher of Will County Weekly Review, one of the best newsmen in Illinois, for his encouragement and direction; without Mr. Cleary's kind attentions, this work would not be possible. I wish to thank Mr. Brian McGrory of the Boston Globe, whose 1995 story about Leo brought some well-earned attention to the Leo Men who remain committed to the values of the parish. Most of all to my Friend and Boss, Bob Foster, whose nearly fifty years of service to this school allowed God's good work to continue on 79th & Sangamon.

Works Cited:

Garraghan, Gilbert J. Catholic Church in Chicago 1673-1871. Loyola University Press. Chicago, IL. 1921.

Kantowicz, Edward R. Corporation Sole: Cardinal Mundelein & Chicago Catholicism. University of Notre Dame Press. Notre Dame, IN. 1983.

Martin, Paul R. The First Cardinal of the West. New World Press. Chicago, IL. 1934.

McMahon, Eileen M. What Parish Are You From? – A Chicago Irish community & Race Relations. University of Kentucky Press. Lexington, KY. 1995.

Schauniger, J. Herman. Profiles in Action: American Catholics in Political Life. The Bruce Publishing Company. Milwaukee, WI. 1966.

Spinney, Robert J. City of Big Shoulders: A History of Chicago. Northern Illinois University Press. DeKalb, IL. 2000.

Primary Sources:

The Lion – Leo High School Yearbook 1930-2004

The Oriole – Leo High School Newspapers 1936-1947

About the Author

Pat Hickey is proud to have been of some service to Leo High School for last ten years.

A native Chicagoan and a career educator, Hickey taught at Bishop McNamara High School, in Kankakee, IL and La Lumiere School, LaPorte, In.   In 1990, he began doing fund-raising work which he continues at Leo High School. Hickey is a tree-lance writer for GAR Media.

Pat Hickey, widowed (Mary) in 1998, is the father of Nora, Conor and Clare Hickey. The Hickey's live in St. Cajetan's Parish in the Morgan Park neighborhood of Chicago.

Spike O'Donnell's 1930 headquarter's called The Highland Building at 7845 S. Ashland (Photo courtesy of Mr. Larry Raeder).

Erected 1926

LEO HIGH SCHOOL

Chicago, Illinois

Conducted by the Christian Brothers of Ireland
UNDER THE PATRONAGE OF HIS EMINENCE GEORGE CARDINAL MUNDELEIN

Thomas Kelly 2H
Fatally Injured

Thomas Kelly

On Sun. May 13 Thomas Kelly,of 2H was struck by an unidentified driver and and died the following morning at St. George's Hospital. Thomas attended St. Sabina's Grammar School and came to Leo in September 1943.

He is survived by his parents Mr. and Mrs. Thomas J. Kelly of 7943 Throop St., his brother Bernard, and two sisters, Loretta and Maureen. Among the pallbearers at his funeral were three Leo sophomores John McGowan, Andrew Sloyan, and Robert McShane.

Printed in the United States
48826LVS00005B/1-6